Setting Up a Limited Company

London: TSO

First published 2001

Second impression 2002

ISBN 0 11 702817 7

Disclaimer

This book put YOU in control. That is an excellent thing, but it also makes YOU responsible for using it properly. Few washing machine manufacturers will honour their guarantee if you don't follow their 'instructions for use'. In the same way, we are unable to accept liability for any loss arising from mistakes or misunderstandings on your part. So please take time to read this book carefully.

This book is not a definitive statement of the law, although we believe it to be accurate and up-to-date as of 1 August 2001. We cannot except liability for changes in the law that take place after the publication date, although every effort will be made to show any such changes on the website.

Contents

About the authors

Mark Fairweather is a practising solicitor, and is one of the founding partners of the legal firm Fairweather Stephenson & Co. He is co-author with Rosy Border of the Stationery Office's *Simply Legal* series of DIY law kits as well as several titles in the *You Need This Book First* series. He has two children and lives in Suffolk.

Rosy Border has worked in publishing, lecturing, journalism and the law. She is a prolific author and adapter who stopped counting after 150 titles. Rosy and her husband, John Rabson, live in Suffolk and have a married son in Tennessee.

Welcome

Welcome to the *You Need This Book First* series. Let's face it – the law is a maze. This book is your map through the parts of the maze that deals with setting up your own limited company. It contains everything lawyers would tell you about this, if only they had time (and you had the money to pay them). And if you follow our advice you should end up with a limited company that

● does what you want it to do

● is legally sound

● you as a non-lawyer can understand.

Acknowledgements

A glance at the *Useful Contacts* section will show how many individuals and organisations we consulted while compiling this book. Thank you, everyone. Individuals whose advice and assistance we gratefully acknowledge include John Oakley, Chartered Accountant of Beatons, Felixstowe, and John Rabson, Chartered Engineer, for his IT support, research and refreshments.

What this book can do for you

This book

- provides general information that professional advisers would give you on the subject, if only they had the time to do so, and if only you had the money to pay them. For example, it tells you what options are available if you are setting up in business for the first time, what it means to be a director, and what paperwork you will have to do

- tells you the buzzwords that are important in this section of the law and what they mean

- tells you what forms are required by law to set up a small private limited company in England or Wales

- tells you what each form is for, so that you not only do all the paperwork correctly but also understand what you are doing and why

- gives you samples of all the letters, resolutions and other documents you will need

- answers some of the most frequently asked questions on the subject

- is supported by a website that is regularly updated. At the time of writing the Government was conducting a review of company law. One of the proposals in this review is the simplification of procedure for company formation so that the only documents needed are a registration form and a constitution.

This book puts *you* in control. That is a good thing; but it means responsibility as well as power. Think of yourself as a driver using a road map. The map tells you the route, but it is up to you to drive carefully along it.

A note about Scotland:

Scotland is a separate jurisdiction from England and Wales, but the procedures for setting up a company are the same, except that the Memorandum of Association (see *Buzzwords)* says 'incorporated in Scotland' instead of 'incorporated in England and Wales'. And Scotland has its own Companies House: The Registrar of Companies, Companies House, 37 Castle Terrace, Edinburgh EH1 2EB, telephone 0131 535 5800.

What this book can't do for you

It can't

- be a textbook. Its job is to help you to set up a limited company, not to teach you the ins and outs of company law. We aim to be streetwise rather than academic

- set up a *public* company. Public companies – that is, the sort of company that is quoted on the Stock Exchange – are outside our remit. This book is confined to small private companies

- help you to set up a company outside England, Wales and (see above) Scotland.

A word of warning

Use this book properly. Read it with care. Take the time to do so – do not skip anything.

- Everything is there for a purpose
- If anything were unimportant, we would have left it out.

There are wide margins in which you can make notes.

We have done our best to provide accurate and up to date information, but laws and regulations can change. This book is based on the law as at 1 August 2001.

This book is suitable for straightforward cases but is no replacement for specific advice you may need on your individual circumstances. For example, we do not give specialist tax advice.

ⓘ–Hazard sign

As with any legal matter, your own common sense will often tell you when you are out of your depth and need expert help. But, in any case, we warn you when you are in danger of getting out of your depth and need to seek professional advice. We will alert you to

● common traps for the unwary

● situations when you are in danger of getting out of your depth and need to take professional advice. Look out for the hazard sign.

ⓘ–Power points

Sometimes we pause to empower you to do something: watch out for the symbol.

Clear English rules OK

We draft WYSIWYG documents – *what you see is what you get.*

Legal documents have traditionally been written in archaic language, because this wording has stood the test of time – often several centuries – and has been hallowed by the courts. What is more, the use of technical language can sometimes enable specialists to express esoteric concepts in a kind of professional shorthand that is useful to them but meaningless to others.

The use of archaic language is, however, unnecessary and may be dangerous. The worst problem is that for non-specialists it is a foreign language, unknown at worst and incompletely understood at best, with all the potential for misunderstanding which that entails. Why write in a foreign language in preference to plain English? Let us all use clear, unambiguous language that accurately reflects our intentions. On the (fairly rare) occasions when we *do* need to use technical language, we offer clear explanations (see *Buzzwords*).

Check out our website

Check out our website, because purchase of this book entitles you to access our exclusive readers' website.

www.youneedthisfirst.co.uk

Buzzwords

Many trades and professions use special words in the course of their work, or use ordinary words in a different way from those outside their own group. For example, a chip does not mean the same to a computer expert as it does to a cook. Eavesdrop on any gathering of doctors, lawyers, plumbers or motor mechanics and you'll see what we mean.

The world of company law is no exception. Here are the companyspeak expressions you will find helpful for setting up your own limited company.

accounting reference date – the date of the company's financial year-end, in other words the date which appears on the company's balance sheet. A new company can set its own accounting reference date by *filing* (see below) Form 225 with Companies House. An accounting reference date, subject to certain restrictions, can be changed in the same way. If no Form 225 is filed, the accounting reference date for a new company will automatically be the last day of the month in which the anniversary of incorporation falls. So, if you set up your company on 1 May, your accounting reference date, unless you state otherwise, will be 31 May.

allotment – the *allocation* of new shares, as opposed to the *transfer* of existing shares. Details of every allotment have to be filed with Companies House on a special form, Form 88(2).

annual general meeting – an annual meeting of shareholders to consider the company's accounts and directors' report.

The first AGM must be held within 18 months of incorporation, and thereafter not more than 15 months can elapse between one AGM and the next. A company can dispense with an AGM by passing an elective resolution to that effect. (A sample minute of elective resolutions is included below and also on our website.)

Annual Return – Form 363A, that has to be filed each year with Companies House.

The Annual Return gives details of the company's shareholders, directors, etc. This is one form that is not downloadable from the Companies House website. Companies House sends it automatically to companies for updating before returning it by post.

Articles of Association – the internal rules of the company – like the constitution of a club.

Certificate of Incorporation – the document issued by Companies House which certifies that the company is registered with them, and which tells you the company number and the date on which the company came into existence. If you change the name of the company (have no fear: we show you how on page 46),

Companies House will issue you with a new certificate of incorporation with the new name.

clear day – a clear day is not necessarily cloudless.

When giving notice of a shareholders' meeting, the notice period is counted in *clear days*, i.e. *excluding* the date the notice is received *and* the date of the meeting. So ten 'clear days' could mean, allowing for the postal services, fourteen 'ordinary days' from the date you send out the notice.

Companies House – the office of the Registrar of Companies, which holds the public records of over one million companies in Great Britain. Its main functions are to

- incorporate and dissolve companies
- examine and hold documents under the Companies Act and related legislation and
- make this information available to the public.

Companies House is at Crown Way, Cardiff, CF4 3UZ; telephone 029 2038 8588; central enquiries, telephone 0870 3333636. It has seven offices nationwide, addresses of which are given in *Useful Contacts*. Companies House also publishes guidance notes, available free of charge.

Companies House is also on-line at: >http://www.companieshouse.gov.uk<. Companies House publishes helpful guidance notes, available free of charge. You will find a list of titles on page 141 and additionally on the website.

company number – the unique number allocated to a company by Companies House.

The company number is like a National Insurance number: you can change your name or the name of the company as often as you like, but the numbers stay the same.

company secretary – the person who is usually made responsible for keeping the company's statutory records and filing (see below) documents with Companies House.

Every company must have a company secretary. See 'Do you really want to be a company secretary?' on page 34.

debenture – strictly speaking, a written acknowledgement of a debt by a company, which may be secured or unsecured. In practice, a debenture refers to a company's secured debt and usually includes a floating charge (see below) and may also include a fixed charge, such as over bricks and mortar.

Scots law on debentures and charges differs from English law on this subject. Consult a solicitor qualified in Scottish law.

dividend – basically, a payment to shareholders of a division or share of a company's profits. Usually a dividend must be recommended by the directors and authorised by a resolution (see below) of the company.

elective resolution – a resolution to dispense with certain formalities.

extraordinary general meeting – see *general meeting*. See our sample minute of elective resolutions on page 73. Elective resolutions are useful for small companies.

filing – sending official documents about the company to Companies House for inclusion on the public register.

Ordinary folk send, submit or even deliver by hand. Companyspeak goes in for filing.

Instead of filing paper documents, you can now make use of

- electronic filing. This is essentially filing by e-mail but before you can do so, you need to register with the Companies House electronic filing service, which will issue you with an authentication code to replace signatures on paper. For further information contact Companies House Direct on telephone 0345 573991 and ask for the free introductory pack.

- Web filing. This is a version of electronic filing, but by way of the Companies House website. To use this service you need a security code and authentication code. For further information access >www.companieshouse.gov.uk< or call the helpline on 029 2038 1393.

floating charge – a charge or mortgage that a company gives over its current or 'floating' assets, such as stock.

Picture a river with the assets floating along like logs in the current. While the water is still liquid – until the floating charge crystallises – the company can buy and sell the assets that are subject to the charge without the lender's permission. If the company defaults on the loan, however, the lender has the right to appoint an administrative receiver. This is the moment when the charge 'crystallises' – that prevents the company from dealing in those assets. Then the river freezes and the logs are stuck in the ice; the assets are frozen. The administrative receiver takes control of them and sells them to repay the debt.

general meeting – a meeting of shareholders. A general meeting that is not an annual general meeting is called an *extraordinary general meeting* even if the business transacted is actually fairly routine.

When a meeting has to be held, proper notice has to be given to everyone entitled to attend unless all (sometimes 95%) consent to short notice. Furthermore, notice of shareholders' meetings should be given to all company directors (even if they are not shareholders) and the company's auditor (if the company has one). The period is counted in *clear days* (see above) – i.e. excluding the day the notice is received and the date of the meeting.

incorporate – to bring (a company) into existence.

issued share capital – the shares actually allotted to the shareholders.

Memorandum of Association – the document that sets out what the company is allowed to do and the powers it has for that purpose. The memorandum also states the company name and other details.

minutes – the permanent written record of shareholders' and directors' meetings and also of any resolution passed without a meeting.

nominal share capital – the shares that a company is allowed to allot to its shareholders, whether it has done so or not.
Nominal share capital is also known as *authorised* share capital. The two are the same.

non-executive director – a director who is not involved in the running of the company on a day to day basis.

ordinary resolution – see under *resolution*.

proxy – a person appointed by a shareholder to vote on their behalf.

A proxy cannot vote on a show of hands (i.e. one vote per *shareholder*), only on a poll (i.e. one vote per *share*) unless the company's articles provide otherwise. The Articles of Association in this book (see page 85) specify 'a show of hands, unless any shareholder present in person or by proxy demands a poll, whether before or after the show of hands'.

proxy notice – a statement on a notice convening a shareholders' meeting, saying that a shareholder can appoint a proxy to attend and vote on their behalf and that the proxy does not have to be a shareholder in the company.

quorum – the minimum number of people needed at a meeting to transact business.

registered office – the address to which official correspondence for the company will be sent. A company's registered office can be different from its *trading* address – they could have a registered office in London and offices and factories worldwide. Wherever else the company is active, its *registered office* must be in England or Wales.

resolution – a formal decision of the shareholders or directors, which must be passed by the appropriate majority. A resolution may be passed on a show of hands (i.e., one vote per *shareholder*) or on a poll (being one vote per *share*). A poll may be demanded before the resolution is put to the vote, or immediately after the result on a show of hands (see also *proxy*).

Instead of calling a meeting, a resolution can be passed – but in this case it has to be unanimous – by getting *everyone* to sign a copy of the resolution (not necessarily the same copy). In the case of a shareholders' written resolution, a draft must be made available to the company's auditor (if the company has one – see pages 42–43). A written resolution normally cannot be used to get rid of a director or an auditor.

All resolutions have to be recorded in writing and some resolutions have to be filed at Companies House.

The basic forms of shareholder resolution are:

1. *Ordinary resolution* – not less than 14 clear days' notice of meeting and a simple majority, in other words over 50%. The notice of meeting must, at least, indicate the general nature of the business to be transacted, and should preferably specify the intended resolution. Copies of some ordinary resolutions have to be filed at Companies House, such as an increase in nominal capital and the dismissal of a director.

2. *Special resolution* – not less than 21 clear days' notice of meeting. The notice *must* specify the intended resolution. The requisite majority is at least 75%. Copies of all special resolutions have to be filed at Companies House.

3. *Elective resolution* – not less than 21 clear days' notice of meeting and unanimous decision. Copies of all elective resolutions have to be filed at Companies House. We show you samples of all three in this book and on the website.

share premium – on an *allotment* (see above) of new shares, the price per share may be greater than the face or nominal value.

When people say 'Cup Final tickets are at a premium' they mean the fans may end up paying £100 for a £10 ticket. That £90 difference is the premium. It's similar with shares – except that it's the company, not a tout, selling its own shares at more than their face value.

special resolution – see *resolution*.

statutory forms – forms which the law requires companies to file (see above) with Companies House.

statutory registers – the registers which the law (*statute* is of course another word for legislation) requires a company to keep.

For a private company these are

● register of members, i.e shareholders

● register of directors and company secretary

● register of directors' interests – i.e., the company's shares and debentures

● register of charges – charges in this context means liabilities such as mortgages and debentures.

subscriber – someone agreeing to take shares in a company.

The subscribers who sign the Memorandum of Association will be the first shareholders in the company.

Table A – the statutory, 'off the peg' form of internal rules of the company which apply by default if a company does not have its own 'customised' rules – that is, rules drafted with that particular company in mind.

The internal rules are known as the *Articles of Association* (see above). The customised rules of a company can use Table A as a starting point, and that is the approach we adopt here. So the Articles of any company formed using this book comprise the customised rules which we include AND Table A as varied by those rules.

The variations we have made to Table A are intended to make the Articles more suitable for a small private company. A professional could look at our Articles, compare them with Table A and say 'Ah yes, they've done so-and-so'. A copy of Table A itself is included in this book (see page 93) and on the website. You do not have to file Table A with Companies House – it has already seen it many times!

Explore your options

Are you at the right party?

This book deals with limited companies. Are you sure you really want to set up a limited company, as opposed to any other kind of business? In other words, 'are you at the right party?'

There are four ways of setting up in business. These are (1) limited company, (2) sole trader, (3) partnership, and (4) limited liability partnership. Each has its pros and its cons. You will need to look at each option carefully before you make up your mind.

1. Limited company

Pros

● *Limited liability.* This means that, as a shareholder in the company, you are not personally liable for the company's debts beyond the amount you are supposed to pay for your shares. Here is how it works. Suppose you have one £1 share with a face, or nominal, value of £1. Then your maximum liability is £1. If, however, you have contracted to pay a *share premium* (see *Buzzwords*), you are liable for the premium as well. Directors do not necessarily get off so lightly, however (see page 31).

And if you are incautious enough to give personal guarantees (such as to the company's bank or landlord) you may end up defeating the whole object of the exercise (see page 31).

● Tax. As a company is a separate legal entity, it pays its own tax on its profits. Individuals pay income tax; companies pay corporation tax, and there are differences in the rules for the two kinds of tax.

Corporation tax starts at just 10% for companies that show a profit of £10,000 or less. If the profits of a single company (not a member of a group of companies) are below £300,000 – the threshold for the tax year 2001–2002 – then the corporation tax rate is still only 20%. The main rate of tax for companies is 30% as of 2001–2002. This applies to profits over £1.5 million. There is what is called 'marginal relief' between the bands – in other words, the increase from one rate of tax to another is applied incrementally. This can work to your advantage, depending on your personal tax situation. If you are a higher rate taxpayer, then you can, by leaving the profits in the company, avoid and/or defer paying higher rate tax.

BUT this advantage is lost if you take the money out of the company, as you will then be taxed at your own rate of tax, because the money is then yours and not the company's.

At the time of writing, there are moves to amend Table A to make it more user-friendly for small companies, but the changes have not yet been made public, far less put into practice.

The tax advantages have encouraged many individuals to sell their services through a limited company to save on tax and National Insurance. The Inland Revenue is well aware of this, and in Inland Revenue announcement IR35 it expressed the intention of cracking down on tax and NI avoidance by people who use companies as a front to provide personal services. If you think this applies to you, seek professional advice.

At the time of writing, there is much passionate discussion among professionals about the effects IR35 is likely to have on small companies. Three websites on which you can read the latest news are

- the Revenue:
  - >www.inlandrevenue.gov.uk/ir35<
- the Tax Zone Digest site:
  - >http://www.taxzone.co.uk<
- the Accounting WEB Newswire site:
  - >http://www.accountingweb.co.uk<
- *Sick pay and other benefits.* If you are an employee of the company, you will qualify for statutory benefits (such as statutory sick pay) like any other employee. The employer company pays these benefits in the first instance, and may then be partly or wholly reimbursed by the government.

—But beware: just being a director is *not* enough to entitle you to statutory benefits. Get yourself a written contract of employment to put your status as employee beyond doubt and to avoid missing out. You can find a suitable contract of employment in the Stationery Office's *Simply Legal* series of law kits. For full details see *Useful Contacts…*

● *Decision-making*. A company is usually a democracy, because decisions are made by vote on a majority basis (although the size of the majority you need depends on circumstances). If you want a limited company but do not want a democracy, seek professional advice. Similarly, if you are or will be a minority shareholder, you may need special protection: seek professional advice.

—● *Borrowing*. It may be easier for a limited company to borrow money, because it can offer the lender security over all its assets in the form of a floating charge (see *Buzzwords*) or debenture (see *Buzzwords*).

● *Investment*. It may be easier for a limited company to attract investors because if they become shareholders, they will have the advantage of limited liability (see above).

● *Continuity*. A company is a separate legal entity from its shareholders, so the company can still go on after a change of shareholders. This may help if a shareholder wants out, retires, becomes insolvent or dies.

- *Transferability.* A company's shares are transferable, although there may be restrictions, for example in the Articles of Association (see *Buzzwords*). Again, this may help if a shareholder wants out, retires, becomes insolvent or dies. In practice, however, it is often difficult to find anyone to buy shares in a private limited company.

- *Dividends.* It is possible to take money out of a company in the form of dividends, thereby avoiding National Insurance contributions.

- *Inheritance Tax.* Shares in private limited companies may qualify for exemption from Inheritance Tax. There are, however, conditions attached – take professional advice.

- *Capital Gains Tax.* Shares in private limited companies may qualify for lower rates of tax on disposal. Again, there are conditions; seek professional advice.

Cons

- *Paperwork.* You have to keep good records, which means either being well organised, or paying someone to do the paperwork for you. Failure to do this will give you a lot of grief (see below).

- *Tax.* There can be circumstances where both the company and its shareholders are liable for tax on the same profit. For example, suppose the company sells an asset at a profit. It then declares a dividend from that profit. In those circumstances, the company pays *corporation tax* on the profit, and the shareholders also pay *income tax* on the dividend. Take professional advice to cushion – or even dodge – the blow.

● *Tax returns*. You will need to submit a tax return for the company as well as for you. If tax returns are not your forte you may need to pay someone to do this for you.

● *National Insurance*. The rate you pay on taking a salary out of the company is higher than the self-employed rate, since the company has to pay both employer's and employee's National Insurance contributions.

● *Costs*. Companies tend to be more expensive to run than other businesses;

● *Rules*. You have to stick to the company's internal rules, known as Articles of Association (see *Buzzwords*). You can't just make up or vary the rules as you go along, although you can change them by a *special resolution* (see resolution under *Buzzwords*) of shareholders.

● *Disclosure*. You have to tell Companies House certain specific information about the company's affairs, which then becomes a matter of public record. If you value your privacy you may not like this, as everyone has the right to inspect your company's file at Companies House.

● *Getting money out*. The company's assets are not *your* assets, so you can't just dip into the cookie jar whenever you feel like it. Note that there is a general ban on loans by a company to its directors, although there is an exception for *small* loans (under £5,000 in aggregate), so this may not bother you too much). Even then, there will be tax to pay.

● *Winding up.* A company is often more complicated and expensive to wind up than other types of business.

● *Professionals.* There are restrictions on people in certain professions making full use of the rules of limited liability. If you think this might apply to you, it is best to take advice from your professional body before setting up the company.

2. Sole trader

Some people are free spirits. Resourceful, self-reliant, they were born to be sole traders. A sole trader is a one-man band. If you are a sole trader, the business is you, and you are the business. You are in charge. You reap the benefits when things go well and you carry the can if things go wrong.

It takes bottle, stamina and a certain amount of luck to prosper as a sole trader. If your health is unreliable, or if business looks like being anything other than brisk, being a sole trader can be a risky undertaking. This is because if you're sick or out of work, you are eligible for fewer benefits (e.g., you would not get statutory sick pay if you fell ill). And if your business gets into trouble, the vultures can take everything you have.

Your business affairs won't be public knowledge in the way a company's are, but you will still have to keep proper accounts and records to stay out of trouble with the taxman and if your turnover is big enough (the current VAT threshold is £54,000) the VAT man too, if for no other reason.

For a small business, being a sole trader is often the right set-up, but it may restrict you when you want to expand. And at that point you can consider putting your business into a company.

3. Partnership

When two or more people get together – Butch Cassidy and the Sundance Kid, Spenlow and Jorkins, Dave Dee, Dozy, Beaky, Mick and Titch – and carry on a business for profit, they have a partnership. The big advantage is that the partners usually share the load of managing the business.

The snag is that *all* the partners are personally liable for the full extent of *all* the debts and mistakes of the business. The magic words are 'jointly and severally liable', which means one partner's misjudgement can ruin the others. If impetuous Spenlow makes a dodgy decision, cautious, sensible Jorkins will suffer equally for it.

An individual partner's liability is not normally limited to the money they themselves have put into the business. *Everything they own may be at risk.*

Unless arrangements are made to the contrary, major partnership decisions – such as decisions affecting the nature of the partnership business – have to be unanimous (literally, of one mind). In the real world, unanimity is hard to achieve and for this reason business partnerships, like marriages, can often end in tears.

4. Limited liability partnership

The limited liability partnership (LLP) is a new kind of business arrangement that came into being on 6 April 2001. In effect, it is hybrid – a cross between a limited company and a partnership. Any new or existing firm of two or more people – except an existing limited company, which would need to do some form filling first – will be able to incorporate (see *Buzzwords*) at Companies House as a limited liability partnership.

An LLP will be taxed as a partnership and its internal structure will be similar to that of a partnership. Members will have to pay Class 2 and Class 4 NI contributions.

Pros

- It gives the partners the protection of limited liability (as in a limited company) although the business itself will be liable for the full extent of its assets. Compared with a traditional partnership, one of the significant benefits of an LLP is that individual partners are not exposed – beyond their stake in the business – to the risk of financial loss caused by the actions of the other partners.

- The partners have the same freedom to organise the internal structure of their business as they would in a traditional partnership. In the context of a small business, this means that the relationship between the partners can be flexible and informal – if that is what they want.

Cons

- As with a company, accounts and an annual return have to be filed with Companies House and be available for public inspection. If privacy is important to you, an LLP is not for you.

- While the liability of the partners will be limited, this may not protect them from the consequences of their own fraud or negligence. For professional partnerships, indemnity insurance will still be vital.

- LLPs are expected to be attractive to professionals such as solicitors and accountants, but their right to make use of LLPs may be restricted by the rules of their profession. (If you think this may apply to you, check with your professional body.)

You can find out more on a special Companies H
website >http://www.startinbusiness.co.uk< that
describes LLPs and answers frequently asked
questions.

There are other business structures available to you,
such as franchises and workers' co-operatives, but
those are outside the scope of this book.

Roles and responsibilities

Let us suppose you decide that a limited company is for you. Before you start downloading the forms from our website and applying to Companies House, you need to step back and look at all the implications of setting up and running a company.

Every limited company must have at least two formally appointed officers. They are

● the company director

● the company secretary.

It should be noted that if you are a sole director – and such animals do exist – you can't be the company secretary as well. There are no one-man-band limited companies.

You don't need any particular academic or professional qualifications to take on either of these roles (see *Frequently asked questions* on page 38), but each role carries its own responsibilities – are you sure you are ready to take them on?

Do you really want to be a company director?

You may believe you will get a buzz out of calling yourself a company director, but you should not become one unless you are prepared to take on the duties and responsibilities of the job.

● **You have less power than you might imagine**

Along with the other directors – collectively known as the board of directors – you are responsible for the management and business of the company. Ultimate power, however, belongs to the shareholders. The board of directors usually has unrestricted power to carry on day to day business, but should otherwise take care not to exceed its authority as set out in the company's Articles of Association (see *Buzzwords*).

● **You can't go it alone**

The board of directors must take decisions collectively, except decisions that it lawfully delegates to someone else, such as a managing director.

● **You must put the company's interests before your own**

You must always do what is best for the company, even if that is not what you want for yourself. You must act in good faith.

You need to be alert to conflicts of interest, and know how to handle them by

1. *disclosing* to the company any personal interest, direct or indirect, that you have in the company's affairs. Do this in writing to the company secretary. Your shares in the company have to be listed in the *Register of Directors' Interests*, which is kept by the company secretary. The same applies to any security you have over the company's assets.

2. *abstaining* from voting on directors' resolutions in which you have a personal interest, unless that interest is of a type where the Articles permit you to vote.

3. *ensuring approval* by the board of directors of all transactions between you and the company. Note that some transactions may need to be approved by the company's shareholders. For example,

    3.1. an employment contract between you and the company for a fixed term of five years or more

    3.2. a substantial property transaction between you and the company

    3.3. a payment to you for loss of office (unless a contractual entitlement under your employment contract).

● **You may end up carrying the can**

Limited liability – that is, liability to the company's creditors – protects *shareholders*, but does not necessarily safeguard *directors*.

As a director you can be made *personally* liable for the company's debts if you allow the company to continue trading when you know – or should know – that it cannot pay its way: in other words, that it is insolvent.

Even if the company is not insolvent, you can sometimes be made personally liable for civil wrongs you yourself commit while on company business. If you were to use the company as a front for fraud, the victims could recover their losses from you personally; you could not use the company as a shield. And, needless to say, if your company commits any criminal offence you can be prosecuted if you were involved.

As if that were not enough, *the company can sue you* if you do not exercise reasonable skill and care in carrying out your duties as a director, or if you commit the company to liabilities without authority from the board.

● **You as a director are personally responsible for the company's accounts**

You must ensure that the company

1. keeps accounting records, ie doing the book-keeping

2. prepares the company's accounts

3. gets the company's accounts audited (if applicable – see *Frequently asked questions* on page 42)

4. presents the accounts to the shareholders, unless they have passed an elective resolution to dispense with this formality (*see elective resolution in Buzzwords*)

5. files the accounts with (i.e. sends them to) Companies House.

The directors also have to prepare an annual report, which must contain certain statutory information and is presented to shareholders and filed with Companies House in the same way as the accounts.

In practice you may well pay someone else to do all this, but it has to be done and you are responsible.

● **You have ultimate responsibility**

For the duties usually taken on by the company secretary (see below). Even if you are paying someone else to do the accounts and/or handle the paperwork, unless certain documents are filed with Companies House on time, *you* take the blame. Failure to file on time or at all is a criminal offence and Companies House can and does prosecute.

● **You could get disqualified**

If your company is wound up, leaving unpaid bills, you may – even if you are not to blame – be

disqualified for a period of time from acting as a
director or a company consultant. This is rather like
losing your driving licence. *Your* name is added to
the *Disqualified Directors' Register* at Companies
House and anyone can apply to see the list, with
your name on it. Even if the company is not wound
up, you may also be disqualified if, in your capacity
as a director, you are guilty of serious wrongdoing,
or even persistent failure to file accounts and other
necessary documents with Companies House (see
also below under *Company secretary*).

● Ignorance is no defence

If you are a director but leave the running of the
company to others (i.e., if you are a non-executive
director), you cannot escape responsibility just
because you do not know what is going on. For this
reason, you should not accept appointment as a non-
executive director unless you are sure you will be
kept fully and regularly informed.

If you do become a director, consider taking out
insurance against the risk of claims against you for
breach of duty. Take advice from an insurance broker
dealing in commercial insurances.

Do you really want to be a company secretary?

Don't confuse a company secretary with the person who does the typing and filing, although in smaller outfits many company secretaries do this in addition to their other duties.

'More kicks than halfpence' is one company secretary's description of the job. A company secretary has no *powers* to speak of, other than to commit the company to contracts of an administrative nature; and no *rights* (unless agreed with the company, e.g. in a contract of employment), but usually takes on the following *duties*:

- Providing shareholders, directors and the company auditor (if there is one – see *Frequently asked questions* on page 42) with written notice of company meetings. There are minimum notice periods (see *resolutions* under *Buzzwords*). The notice must say what the meeting is to be about – in practice, an agenda – and it must include the draft wording of any special or elective resolution(s). (In practice, of course, it is always sensible to include the draft wording of any resolution.) There must be a proxy notice (see *Buzzwords*).

- Distributing copies of the company's accounts not less than 21 days before meetings at which the accounts will be discussed. The company secretary must send copies to: shareholders, directors and debenture holders.

● Keeping minutes of shareholders' and directors'
  meetings (which means of course that the company
  secretary must attend the meetings and take notes,
  then get them typed up and circulated afterwards).

● Ensuring that certain statutory forms (see
  Buzzwords) are filed with Companies House on
  time. A letter is not enough: you have to file the
  correct form. The main forms – and this is not an
  exhaustive list – are

  ○ 288a, 288b and 288c – changes of director or
    company secretary or alteration of their
    registered details (e.g. home address). The form
    must be filed *within 14 days* of the change;

  ○ 363A – the annual return, which Companies
    House sends automatically to each company and
    which must be filed *within 28 days* of the date of
    the information supplied in the return. (All the
    forms are available on the Companies House
    website at http://www.companieshouse.gov.uk)

● Filing copies of certain resolutions with Companies
  House. All *elective* and *special resolutions* (see
  Buzzwords) have to be filed. Ordinary resolutions
  do not usually have to be filed – but there are
  exceptions, such as increase in nominal capital and
  dismissal of a director. The resolutions have to be
  filed *within 15 days* of the date on which they were
  passed.

● Maintaining the statutory registers (see *Buzzwords*)

● Filing accounts with Companies House (strictly speaking, this is the directors' job, but tends to get delegated either to the company secretary or the auditor – if there is one: see *Frequently asked questions* on page 42)

Criminal liability

A company secretary is not normally involved in the management or business of the company (unless, of course, as often happens, they are also a director). However, *a company secretary is an officer of the company and may therefore be held criminally liable* along with the directors if certain documents (such as the annual return or changes to the directors'/company secretary's registered details) are not filed on time – or at all – with Companies House (see above).

Frequently
asked
questions

Do I have to set up the company myself?

No. Apart from using this book and the website that goes with it, there are three other ways of setting up a company. These are

- buying an off-the-shelf company. Look out for ads in the business section of your newspaper. If you do this, make sure that the company has not traded before you take it over. Why worry? Well, for example, if you bought an existing company with a big debt outstanding, all the profits that the company earns through your efforts might go to paying it off.

Most formation agents provide a certificate of non-trading.

- paying a professional to do it for you – the operative word here is *paying*!

- getting an introductory pack from Companies House. Call 0870 3333636. It is also accessible at >http://www.companieshouse.gov.uk<

(FAQS) — **Can I call my company anything I want to?**

No. See *Name this company* on page 51.

(FAQS) — **Can I start trading before the company is set up?**

Yes, but you can be made *personally* liable for all contracts and commitments you make before the date on your certificate of incorporation.

(FAQS) — **Do I have to be a shareholder to be a director?**

No.

Can I run the company without being a director?

Not really. If the buck stops with you, then you really should accept formal appointment as a director. A person pulling the strings behind the scenes is called a shadow director and has the same duties and liabilities as a director who has been formally appointed. A paid manager, answerable to the directors, does not him/herself have to be a director.

(FAQS) — **Do I need any qualifications to be a company director?**

No, but

● you must have the mental capacity to be able to consent to your appointment and

● you must not be a disqualified person, such as an undischarged bankrupt, or a person against whom a disqualification order has been made.

Are there any upper or lower age limits on directors?

There is no upper age limit for directors of *private* limited companies. The test is mental capacity – they can serve for as long as they can understand the obligations, etc., of the appointment. A director of a *public* limited company who is 70 or over cannot accept appointment for the first time unless the appointment is approved by an ordinary resolution of shareholders, although serving directors can be *reappointed* beyond that age.

There is no lower age limit for directors in England and Wales. Again, the test is mental capacity (which is why some teenage whizz-kids have their own companies before they are allowed to drive a car).

Do I need any qualifications to be a company secretary?

No, unless you are the company secretary of a public company. Literacy and numeracy are important, however – how otherwise could you keep Companies House happy?

Can I pay a professional to do the paperwork for me – for example, filing statutory forms and accounts?

Yes, certainly; but *you* remain ultimately responsible.

To quote Companies House, 'ACCOUNTANTS AND FINANCIAL ADVISERS DON'T GET PROSECUTED OR PENALISED. YOU DO'.

Do I have to keep the minutes of meetings on paper, and do I have to have a minute book?

No and no. But you do have to keep minutes, and the legal requirement, in effect, is that they must be in a form from which a readable version can be made and kept available for inspection at your registered office.

You can, therefore, keep your minutes on a computer or, it seems, even a tape recorder, as long as you are able to guard against falsification and have the ability to detect false entries. A paper copy of your minutes, signed by the chairman of the meeting, is good evidence of what went on. Traditionally, the paper copy is kept in a bound minute book; and you can buy one – at some expense – from any business stationer. Alternatively, if your minutes are on paper, you can use a lever arch file; but again, the law expects you to guard against falsification.

You can overcome the requirement for minutes as such by not holding a meeting. Remember the alternative, which is to pass resolutions by getting everyone to sign them (see page 13). A paper record will, however, be unavoidable, because the law does not yet recognise electronic signatures.

—Can I file forms with Companies House from my computer instead of on paper?

Yes. You can use the Companies House electronic filing service or their web filing service (see *filing* in *Buzzwords*).

How many shareholders does the company need? ——— (FAQS)

One, but in that case you must insert a statement in the
register of shareholders that the company has only one
shareholder.

How many directors does the company need? ——— (FAQS)

One, but a sole director cannot also be the company
secretary. If you are a sole director, you are supposed to
keep written records of all contracts between you and
the company.

Does the company need a managing director? ——— (FAQS)

No.

Does the company need a chairman? ——— (FAQS)

No.

Can I advertise for shareholders? ——— (FAQS)

No, not unless you provide a prospectus that complies
with the Public Offers of Securities Regulations 1995
(as amended) or one of the exemptions from the
Regulations applies. The main exemption is an offer or
advertisement specifically addressed to no more than
50 people. This is an arcane area of the law. Seek
professional advice, as breach of the Regulations is a
criminal offence.

FAQs —Do the shareholders have to hold an annual general meeting?

Yes, unless they pass an *elective resolution* (see *Buzzwords*) not to do so.

FAQs —Apart from the AGM, do the shareholders have to hold meetings?

No, unless they need to pass a resolution. Even then, they can dispense with a meeting if they *all* agree and *all* sign the resolution they want to pass.

FAQs —Must company accounts be audited?

Size matters! The general rule is that company accounts must be audited.

But this does not usually apply to a company that qualifies as a 'very small company', that is to say, a company whose balance sheet total is not more than £1.4 million, and whose turnover is not more than £1 million. If your company is a charity, to qualify for total exemption from audit its gross income must be not more than £90,000 and its balance sheet total not more than £1.4 million.

There are, however, categories of 'very small company' whose accounts must still be audited. For example, some flat management companies may have to prepare audited accounts to comply with the terms of their lease. Another example would be a trading company which is part of a *group* of companies where the *group* balance sheet total turnover exceeds the 'very small company' limits.

This can be a complex area; for further details, seek professional advice. Bear in mind that in practice you may still need audited accounts even if it is not a legal requirement. For example, you may find that the company's bank is reluctant to lend money to the company unless the accounts have been audited. Moreover, 10% by value of the company's shareholders can in any case demand an audit.

Even if your accounts need not be audited, remember that you will still have to keep accounting records and maintain proper accounts as you still have to file accounts with Companies House and you need them for tax purposes.

Does the company need an auditor?

Only if its accounts have to be audited (see above).

Must all companies file accounts at Companies House?

Yes, without exception – including those that do not need their accounts audited. But small companies may be entitled to file abbreviated accounts.

The criteria are:

1. The company's asset total is not more than £1.4 million

2. Its turnover is not more than £2.8 million;

3. Its average number of employees is not more than 50.

The company must still, however, provide a fuller set of accounts for shareholders and the Inland Revenue.

— What else does the company have to file at Companies House?

Plenty! The following list is not exhaustive:

- the annual return (form 363a);

- appointments and resignations of directors and company secretary (and their changes of address etc.) – forms 288a, 288b, 288c;

- share allotments – form 88(2);

- some types of *resolution* (see *Buzzwords*);

- changes of registered office address;

- details of mortgages;

- details of insolvency procedures.

— What is the best way to invest in the company?

This will depend on individual circumstances, and if in doubt you should seek professional advice.

— However, it's often best to lend money to the company rather than to subscribe for shares. This is because loans can be secured on the company's assets (e.g., by floating charge; see *Buzzwords*) and are easier to get back than share capital.

— What is the best way to get money out of the company?

This too will depend on individual circumstances, and again if in doubt you should seek professional advice.

Do I need a company seal?

No. But you can have one if you want.

What does the company have to put on its official stationery?

The following:

- the company name, exactly as it appears on its Certificate of Incorporation (see *Buzzwords*), including the word 'limited' – the latter is vital to maintain limited liability;

- the company's country of registration – which will be England or Wales;

- the company's registered number – the one on the Certificate of Incorporation;

- the company's registered office address;

- either the names of *all* the directors, or *none* of them. Surnames are obligatory, but initials may be used instead of forenames.

And what happens if the company name is missed out (e.g., because it has a different trade name) or is not given in full?

The company and those of its directors/company secretary who are responsible can be fined and may be made personally liable for the company's debts.

— Does the company need to display its name anywhere?

Yes – on its official stationery (see above). The name only must be displayed on the outside of its registered office and (if different) all places of business where people can read it.

—Can the name of the company be changed?

Yes. You will need a special resolution. See the sample minute of extraordinary general meeting to change the company name on page 76 and on the website.

You then send a copy of the resolution to Companies House with a fee of £10. It will send you a new *Certificate of Incorporation* (see *Buzzwords*), and the change of name takes effect from the date on the new certificate.

— If you are in a tearing hurry to change the company name, Companies House offers a same-day service for £80 – reduced from £100 on 1 April 2001. Call the helpline on 029 2038 0929 before 3 p.m. with your credit card number and they'll tell you how to do it by close of business that day.

—Can the company trade under a different name from its registered name?

Yes, but you must still include the registered name and other details (see above) on the company's official stationery and display the registered name at the registered office and places of business.

Can the Articles of Association be changed?

Yes. You will need a *special resolution* (see *Buzzwords*), which you send to Companies House with a copy of the amended Articles, signed by one of the directors. There is no fee for this service.

Can the objects of the company as stated in the Memorandum of Association be changed?

Yes, as for change of Articles of Association, above. And, as before, there is no fee.

Can directors be added or removed?

Yes. Adding is easy. Directors can always be appointed by resolution of the company. The Articles of Association usually, however, allow the board of directors to appoint an additional director who remains in office until the next annual general meeting, when the appointment is confirmed (or not). Remember to complete Form 288a and file it with Companies House.

Unless they disqualify themselves, directors who do not want to resign can usually only be removed by the shareholders. The procedure is complicated, and you will need professional advice.

Some companies have the equivalent of the 'black spot' in their Articles of Association: a director must resign forthwith if notice in writing is given to them and signed by all other directors.

Notifying Companies House of the resignation of a director or company secretary is done on Form 288b.

FAQS —**Can I incorporate my company electronically?**

The law has been changed as from 22 December 2000 and now allows you to do this, but Companies House has not yet (at the time of writing) got the practical arrangements in place.

It does, however, expect to make this service available to members of the public by March 2002. For further information check out Companies House website on >www.companieshouse.gov.uk<.

FAQS —**I have heard of shareholders' agreements. Do I need one?**

There is no statutory requirement. All the same, shareholders' agreements are common, and are particularly useful where there are two or more shareholders (you would hardly need one if you were the only shareholder!) and:

● one or more of them are minority shareholders who want to limit the powers of the majority;

● one or more of them are investors who want an exit route if, for whatever reason, they want to take their money and run.

—A shareholders' agreement is not a DIY job, and if your company has a professional investor on board they are likely to impose one on you anyway! Take professional advice.

My business colleague and I ordered £1,000 of goods
before setting up our company. We haven't paid the
supplier yet. Can we make him invoice the company
instead of us?

No, unless the supplier agrees this either at the time of
the contract, or later. Otherwise, you and your business
colleague are personally liable to the supplier.
A separate issue concerns whether you can reclaim the
expense from the company: Yes, as long as the
company receives the benefit of the contract– ie. gets
the goods.

I am setting up a new company, and intending to
give small shareholdings to employees. Are there any
potential problems I should know about?

Yes. Think ahead to what you expect to happen if and
when the employee leaves – and starts working for your
main rival. You need a mechanism to get the shares
back, and you need it in place before you start giving
your shares away! Take professional advice.

My colleague and I are setting up a limited
company. He insists that he should have 51% of the
shares and I should take 49%. He says that just two
shares won't make any real difference. Should I go
along with what he wants?

No, at least not without understanding the implications
of what you are doing. Remember that a company is a
democracy (or a dictatorship of the majority, depending
on your point of view) – and having 51% of the shares
therefore gives effective control. The law does provide

a degree of protection for minority shareholders, but it
is weak. If you own the shares on a fifty-fifty basis
there is the risk of deadlock if you cannot agree, but
that will almost certainly be better than having
decisions imposed upon you that you disagree with. If
these issues arise, take legal advice.

Name this company

Choosing a snappy name is only half the story.
You must also make sure you are allowed to use that
name. Here is your checklist. A company name

- *must* have the word 'limited' at the end of it
  (although there are exceptions for certain non-
  profit-making companies which do not have shares).
  If the company's registered office is in Wales you
  can use 'Cyfyngedig' instead, but in that case you
  must (for the benefit of non-Welsh speakers) state in
  English on the company's stationery and nameplate
  that the company is limited;

- *must not* be *exactly* the same as any name which is
  already registered with Companies House.
  Companies House will check this for you free of
  charge. See below for how to do this;

- *must not* be offensive or criminal;

- *must not* mislead the public concerning the
  company's activities. Take care with names which
  suggest a grand scale of enterprise or impressive
  connections when this is not matched by reality
  (such as Trotter's International Trading Company
  Limited);

- *must not* give the public the idea that the company
  is connected with the government, a local authority
  or royalty;

- *must* not use any of a list of 'sensitive' words
  without permission. These are too numerous to list
  here. The Companies House guidance leaflet,
  GBF2, includes a list of these words and details of
  where to go for permission to use them.

Furthermore, although your choice of name may be
acceptable to Companies House, it may not be
acceptable to others. Do not tread on other people's
toes, particularly people in the same line of business as
yourself, who may take legal action if they think your
choice of name is so close to theirs that the public
might not be able to tell the difference.
Examples:

Virginal Airlines Limited
Cocoa Cola Limited
Stationary Office Publishing Limited

Check out the names

Before you make your final choice of name, do a name
search at Companies House:

On-line: Companies House offers an on-line search
facility at >http://www.companieshouse.gov.uk<. Check
your choice against the list of names on the website.

By telephone: Companies House will do a telephone
search for you. Call its general helpline on 0870
3333636 to find out then and there if your choice of
name has already been registered.

A subtle change may get you there: If your chosen name is already in use, Companies House will advise you over the telephone (see above) whether a subtle alteration (e.g., from Smith Enterprises to Smith's Enterprises) will get you what you want.

● For more detailed guidance on choosing a name, see the Companies House leaflet GBF2, *Company Names*. If in doubt, you can also seek advice from the Companies House helpline, 0870 3333636 as above.

Check out the trade marks

Many attractive company names are registered as trade marks – and are therefore protected. Do you really want to give your company a name that someone else owns and may go to law to defend? Before making your final choice of company name, consider seriously making a search of the Trade Marks Index.

There are two ways of conducting a search:

● The expensive but very thorough way is to let the Patent Office's Central Enquiry Unit Search and Advisory Service (SAS) do it for you. Contact it on telephone 01633 811010, fax 01633 811020, e-mail >commercialsearches@patent.gov.uk<. It aims to turn requests around within seven working days. A trade mark search plus advice will, however, cost you £82.25 including VAT.

● The free way is through a link from the Companies House website >www.companieshouse.gov.uk< to the Trade Marks Database Enquiry and you can do an on-line search for free. However, it is a blunt instrument that is limited to trade marks identical to the ones you type in or trade marks starting with the character you type in. So 'Phonehome' might not be listed, but 'Fonehome' might be; and the owners of that trade mark would be justifiably aggrieved if you registered a trade mark so similar to theirs.

Claim your domain

It is sensible to choose a company name that can also be a domain name – that is, one you can use on a website.

Domain names are allocated on a first-come-first-served basis – so you cannot have your choice of name if someone else has got there before you. To do a domain name search, access the Companies House website and click on its 'domain name' link. This will take you to Nominet, which says 'Companies House holds authoritative records for company registrations, DVLA for driving licences, Nominet maintains the database for registered internet names'. Use the WHO IS facility to check whether your chosen domain name is available, then click on 'How to Register'.
You can register either direct through Nominet at £80 per name plus VAT or through a Nominet member, typically your Internet service provider.

You may find to your annoyance that someone else has beaten you to register your favourite name. If they have no proper use for the name, you may be the victim of a 'cyber-squatter'.

Setting up your company

This book provides everything you need to set up a private limited company in England or Wales, organised as follows:

- One or more directors to manage the company;
- A company secretary (who can be a director but *not* the only director);
- Nominal share capital (see *Buzzwords*) of £10,000 made up of 10,000 shares of £1 each.

Have no fear! This does *not* mean you actually need to put £10,000 into the company – the nominal share capital represents the shares you are allowed to allot. You can form your company with a minimum of one share – so if this share has a nominal value of £1, the liability of the subscriber (i.e. first shareholder) is limited to £1.

- A registered office in England or Wales (see note on page 2 concerning Scotland).

Here is a checklist of the documents you will need:

1. Memorandum of Association

The form of Memorandum in this book and on the website follows convention and assumes there are two subscribers (see *Buzzwords*) – but there can be just one, and there can be more than two. Companies House *cannot* supply you with this document. We do!

2. Articles of Association

This document sets out the regulations concerning the running of the company and is not available from Companies House (see page 85 for our version).

The Articles in this book are based on Table A (see *Buzzwords*), but we have made several important changes to make them more suitable for a small business. These are:

- Shares cannot be transferred unless they are first offered to existing shareholders. This is technically called pre-emption.

- Directors are not required to stand down periodically and apply for re-election (technically called retirement by rotation).

- The person chairing meetings does *not* have a second casting vote.

- The company can have just one shareholder.

- The company can have just one director and there is no maximum number of directors.

- Directors can hold meetings by telephone video conference or internet relay chat room.

- Directors can vote even where there is a conflict of interest (although the interest must always be disclosed and the director must vote for what is best for the company).

- Directors can provide themselves with pensions and life and sickness insurance.

- Written notices can be sent by post, fax, e-mail or short text message.

- The directors are given the power to take out insurance to protect themselves from any liabilities they may incur in carrying out their duties.

What we have provided here, in the Articles, is an off-the-peg product. But there are often circumstances where what you need is a tailor made garment. If in doubt, seek professional advice.

3. Form 10

This form gives details of:

- first directors
- first company secretary
- address of the registered office.

4. Form 12

This form confirms that the directors have gone through the proper procedures to form the company.

We also include a sample covering letter to Companies House.

How to fill in the forms

You can have as many dry runs as you like. Just download extra forms from the Companies House website.

Complete the forms by

● typing, or

● writing with *black* ink in *block capitals*, or

● on the computer.

– Companies House now has an on-line form service at >http://www.companieshouse.gov.uk<. Access this, click on 'Forms' and you can download them, and complete the forms on your computer. To complete the forms on line you will need an up-to-date version of Adobe Acrobat, which you can download free of charge from the Companies House website.

Although you can access the forms and fill them in on line, you will still have to print out the completed forms for signing (both forms) and for completing the declaration (Form 12).

Document quality is important to Companies House, because it scans the forms to produce an electronic image from which to work. Photocopies of forms are generally not acceptable. If in doubt, contact Companies House.

1. Memorandum of Association

Our version is supplied on page 83 and on the website.

Fill in

● the company's name in the *two* spaces provided

● the number of shares to be taken by each subscriber, and the total number of shares

● the names and addresses of the subscribers.

The subscribers now *sign* the Memorandum *in front of an adult witness* who then signs the Memorandum, adding their name and address. (It is not sufficient for the subscribers to witness each other's signatures, but there is nothing to stop a relation from being a witness.)

Date the Memorandum on the day it is signed.

2. Articles of Association

Our version is supplied on page 85 and on our special website.

Fill in the name of the company on the top of the form. The subscribers must also *sign* the Articles, and their signatures are witnessed as above.

Date the Articles with the same date as the Memorandum.

3. Form 10

The last page of Form 10 gives notes for guidance on how it should be completed, and we recommend you read those notes before filling in the form.

Fill in

● the company name in full

● the address of the registered office, including postcode

● a contact name, address and telephone number for queries (which might be different from the registered address).

There is a space here on the form for a DX number. The DX is a private postal system operated mainly by lawyers, banks, etc. It isn't obligatory: ignore if you don't have one.

● full name and usual residential address, including postcode, of the company secretary

- for each director:

  1. full name

  2. usual residential address, including postcode

  3. date of birth

  4. nationality

  5. business occupation (be specific – 'company director' will *not* do) AND

  6. details of any other directorships currently held, or held in the last five years. (If the answer is none, say NONE).

Remember that an undischarged bankrupt or a disqualified person cannot be a director. Luckily it is simple to check 'em out:

Bankrupts: call the Insolvency Service on 020 7637 1110 and they will tell you immediately over the phone whether an individual is bankrupt (or is subject to bankruptcy proceedings).

Disqualified directors: Call the Companies House *Disqualified Directors Register* on the general helpline 0870 3333636 giving the person's surname and initial; they can usually check over the telephone.

While bankruptcy disqualifies anyone from being a director, an individual voluntary arrangement (IVA – a form of private bankruptcy) does not.

The form now has to be *signed*

● by the company secretary, to confirm their consent to act

● by each of the directors, to confirm their consent to act

● by each of the subscribers who signed the Memorandum, or by an agent acting for them.

Now *date* the form with the same date as the Memorandum and the Articles.

4. Form 12

Form 12 is a declaration that the statutory requirements necessary to form a company have been complied with. The form has to be signed in front of a solicitor or, if you can find one, a Justice of the Peace. The solicitor will charge a fee of £5. Before signature

● insert the name of the company

● insert your own name and usual residential address

● make the appropriate deletions to say in what capacity (such as 'director') you are signing the form.

After signing, insert the date – which must not be a date before the one on Form 10 and the Memorandum of Association and Articles of Association. The same date or a later date will be fine.

Make sure you get the company name exactly right in ——
all the documents and that it includes the word
'Limited'.

Next steps

● Take photocopies of all the completed forms to keep
  with the minute book (the originals will be retained
  at Companies House).

● Prepare your covering letter to Companies House –
  see our sample.

Write your cheque, made payable to Companies House.
The fee is £20 at the time of going to press. To confirm
the current fee, call the Companies House helpline on
0870 3333636. Send the forms to Companies House at

New Companies Section
Companies House
Crown Way
Cardiff, CF4 3UZ.

Checklist:

Form 10
Form 12
Memorandum of Association
Articles of Association
Cheque for £20
Covering letter

In return, Companies House will send you your
Certificate of Incorporation. This normally takes 7–14
days.

–If you are in a tearing hurry to get your company off the ground, Companies House offers a same-day incorporation service for £80 (reduced from £100 from April 1 2001) instead of the usual £20.

There are two ways of doing this. You can deliver the papers, and a cheque for £80 made out to Companies House, by hand to your nearest Companies House office (it has outposts at Leeds, London and Birmingham as well as Cardiff – see *Useful Contacts* for details).

The other way is to send everything by first class mail, marking the envelope URGENT SAME DAY. Provided Companies House receives the incorporation papers before 3 p.m. on a working day, the company will be incorporated on the same day and the certificate will be sent to you by return of post.

And now ... you have a shiny new company

These are the first steps you should consider taking. Our sample minutes of first meeting of directors (see page 69) will give you further guidance.

Allot further shares. Remember to file Form 88(2) (available on line from the Companies House website) with Companies House, and to complete details in the register of allotments and register of members (shareholders). The shareholders should be issued with share certificates (see sample certificate on page 82). If shares are allotted to directors, they should notify their respective interests to the company and the interest should be noted in the register of directors' interests.

Remember that the directors cannot allot shares beyond the nominal capital – which our specimen documents set at £10,000. If you want to allot shares for more than £10,000, either ensure that your Memorandum of Association provides a higher nominal capital, or pass a shareholders' ordinary resolution (see *Buzzwords*) to increase the nominal capital. A copy of this resolution must be filed with Companies House together with Form 123.

Additionally, the directors must have authority for the allotment. We provide for this in our specimen Articles of Association, but limited to £10,000. The authority expires after five years (the statutory maximum).

● Choose a bank.

—Many banks will give new businesses an introductory period of free banking. Shop around and see who will offer you the best deal.

● Appoint auditors (if you need them – see *Frequently asked questions)*;

● Fix an accounting reference date (see *Buzzwords*); remember you have to file Form 225 with Companies House.

Pass an elective resolution (see *Buzzwords*) to dispense with formalities (see sample on page 73)

Sample letters, minutes and resolutions

The documents that follow are examples only. On the website that supplements this book, the names, addresses, dates and any fictitious details are highlighted for you to change according to your needs.

The documents are:

Covering letter to Companies House

Sample minutes of first meeting of directors

Sample minutes of elective resolutions

Sample notice of extraordinary general meeting of shareholders

Sample minutes of extraordinary general meeting

Sample written resolution of shareholders

Sample written resolution of directors

Sample share certificate

Covering letter to Companies House

[From:Philip Pirrip
The Old Forge
Rochester
Kent]

The Registrar of Companies
Companies House
Crown Way
Cardiff CF14 3UZ

[date]

Dear Sir

[Great Expectations Limited]

We wish to set up a new company whose main business will be [the manufacture and sale of maternity wear]. We enclose:

>Memorandum of Association
>Articles of Association
>Form 10
>Form 12
>Cheque for £20 in payment of the registration fee.

We look forward to receiving our certificate of incorporation.

Yours faithfully

[Philip Pirrip]

Sample minutes of first meeting of directors

[Heathcliff Enterprises Limited]

Company Number: _____

Minute of Directors' Meeting

Place of meeting: [Wuthering Heights, Haworth, Yorkshire]

Date and time: [1 January] (year) at [9 a.m.].

Directors Present: [Hindley Earnshaw, Catherine Earnshaw, Edgar Linton]:

Others present: [Ellen Dean, company secretary]

1. Documents

The following documents were produced to the meeting:

1.1   the certificate of incorporation

1.2   the Memorandum and Articles of Association

1.3   Form 10, as filed at Companies House

1.4   bank forms: mandate and resolution to appoint bank.

2. Report

The company had been formed by the subscribers named on the Memorandum of Association, and the first directors, the first company secretary and the registered office were as stated in Form 10.

3. Declarations of interests

[Catherine Earnshaw], as a director of [Moorland Construction Limited], declared [her] – interest in a proposed contract with the company [to make Wuthering Heights into a heritage theme park].

4. Auditors

It was resolved to appoint [Lockwood and Co.] as the company's auditors, and that their remuneration would be fixed by the directors.

[or]

It was reported that the company would be a small company for accounting purposes and that it would not be necessary to appoint an auditor.

5. Bank

5.1   It was resolved to appoint [Joseph's Bank plc] as the company's bank.

5.2   The company secretary was instructed to complete the bank forms and arrange for them to be signed.

6. Accounting reference date

6.1   It was resolved that the company's accounting reference date should be _____

6.2   The company secretary was instructed to file Form 225 (notice of accounting reference date) with Companies House.

7. Allotment of shares

7.1   It was resolved to allot ordinary shares of £1 each in the capital of the company [including subscriber shares] for cash at par as follows:

[Heathcliff International Trading plc (HIT) – 98 shares

Hareton Earnshaw – 1 share

Edgar Linton – 1 share]

7.2   The company secretary was instructed to enter the names of the shareholders in the Register of Members, to issue share certificates to the shareholders and to file Form 88 (2) with Companies House.

8 Notice of directors' interests in shares or debentures

8.1   The company secretary reported that she had received written notice from the following directors of their respective interests in shareholdings in the company:

[Hindley Earnshaw – 1 ordinary share of £1, held by his son

Hareton Earnshaw

Edgar Linton – 1 ordinary share of £1.]

8.2 The company secretary was instructed to record these shareholdings in the Register of Directors' Interests.

9 Business
It was resolved to enter into a contract with [Moorland Construction Limited to build a theme park].

10 Conclusion
The meeting ended at [10 30 a.m.].

_____

Director

Sample minute of elective resolutions

The purpose of elective resolutions is to reduce the formalities with which private limited companies have to comply. Without them, companies must

- hold annual general meetings
- lay accounts and reports before general meetings
- if they need an auditor, appoint one annually instead of letting their appointment continue indefinitely.

Without an elective resolution to the contrary, the authority of directors to allot shares is limited to five years (see Articles of Association).

An elective resolution requires not less than 21 clear days' notice unless all shareholders agree otherwise. Notice of the elective resolution should be sent to shareholders and also to all directors and the company auditor (if there is one). An elective resolution must be passed unanimously by all shareholders entitled to attend and vote, and after it is passed a copy must be put in the minute book and a copy filed at Companies House.

[Gradgrind Realities Limited]

Company Number: _____

Minute of shareholders' meeting

Place of meeting: [Slagheap Hall, Coketown]

Date and time: [1 January] (year) at [9 a.m.].

Directors Present: [Thomas Gradgrind, Josiah Bounderby, Sam Sleery],being all the shareholders in the company

Others present: [Mrs Sparsit, company secretary]

1. Consent to short notice

The shareholders unanimously confirmed their consent to holding the meeting on short notice.

2. Annual general meeting

It was resolved to dispense with the holding of annual general meetings.

3. Accounts

It was resolved to dispense with laying accounts and reports before general meetings of the company.

4. Auditors

It was resolved to dispense with the annual appointment of auditors.

5. Directors' authority to allot shares

It was resolved that

● section 80(a) of The Companies Act 1985 shall apply and

● the directors have authority for an indefinite period to allot shares in the capital of the company up to a maximum amount of £10,000.

6. Filing

The company secretary was instructed to file a copy of these resolutions with Companies House within 14 days.

_____

Director

Sample notice of extraordinary general meeting of shareholders

Remember that the length of notice depends on the type of resolution, unless the shareholders consent to short notice (for further details see general meeting in *Buzzwords*). A copy of the notice should be sent to the company's auditor (if it has one) and directors as well as to all shareholders. As an alternative to holding a meeting, you may find it easier to use written resolutions signed by all shareholders (see sample below).

[Pickwick Papers Limited]

Company Number: _____

You are invited to a meeting of the company's shareholders

Place: [the White Horse Hotel, Ipswich, Suffolk]

Date and time: [date] at [time]

The purpose of the meeting is to consider and, if thought fit, pass the following resolution as a special resolution:

The name of the company be changed to [Pickwick Electronic Archives Limited].

Date _____
By order of the board

_____
Company secretary

A member entitled to attend and vote at the meeting is entitled to appoint a proxy to attend and vote in their place. The proxy need not be a member of the company.

Sample minute of extraordinary general meeting

[Pickwick Papers Limited]

Company Number: _____

Minute of a general meeting of the company

Place: [the White Horse Hotel, Ipswich, Suffolk]

Date and time: [date] at [time].

Shareholders present: [Mr Samuel Pickwick, Mr Augustus Snodgrass, Mr Nathanial Winkle, Mrs Eliza Bardell.].

Others Present: [Mr Samuel Weller, company secretary].

1. The chairman announced that a quorum was present and that all shareholders had consented to short notice of the meeting.

2. The company secretary reported that [he had carried out an on-line search at the Companies House website, and that the name Pickwick Electronic Archives Limited was available. He had also checked the Trade Marks Index and no such name was registered. Moreover, the name Pickwick Electronic Archives was also available as a domain name].

3. IT WAS RESOLVED as a special resolution that:

the name of the company be changed to [Pickwick Electronic Archives Limited].

4 The company secretary was instructed to file a copy of the resolution with Companies House, and to pay the fee of £10 to Companies House for a new certificate of incorporation on change of name. The company secretary was also instructed to order new stationery.

5 There being no other business, the meeting closed at [time].

Date_____
By order of the board

_____

Company secretary

Sample written resolution of shareholders

A written resolution can be used instead of holding a meeting, as long as it is signed by *all* the shareholders. However, written resolutions cannot be used to remove a director or auditor before their term of office expires. Remember that a copy of the resolution in draft form should be sent to the company's auditor (if the company has one). Within seven days of receiving the draft resolution, the auditor can ask the shareholders to hold a meeting instead of dealing with the matter in writing. And all special and elective resolutions and some ordinary resolutions have to be filed with Companies House.

[Scrooge and Marley Limited]

Company Number: _____

Resolution of the shareholders passed on [date]:

[That in view of the increase in the pay of Mr Robert Cratchit, clerk, to comply with recent minimum wage legislation, no dividend be declared this year.]

Signatures of all shareholders:

....
[Ebenezer Scrooge]

....
[Jacob Marley]

Sample written resolution of directors

The purpose of a written resolution is to dispense with holding a meeting. The resolution has to be signed by *all* the directors.

[Scrooge and Marley Limited]

Company Number: _____

Resolution of the directors passed on [date]:

[That the wages of Mr Robert Cratchit, Clerk, be increased in accordance with the new minimum wage legislation by the absolute minimum required by the law and a charge be levied for lighting and heating his garret].

....
[Ebenezer Scrooge]

....
[Jacob Marley]

Sample share certificate

Share Certificate number [1]

[Scrooge and Marley Limited]

This certificate records that the shareholder is registered in the company's share register as the holder of the following shares:

Name of Shareholder: [Jacob Marley]

Nominal value of each share: [£1]

Number of shares to which this certificate entitles the shareholder: [10]

Total nominal value of shares to which this certificate entitles the shareholder: [£10]

Executed by the company acting by:

signature of **director** ....

signature of **director** or **company secretary** ....

Date ....

Memorandum, Articles and Table A

Memorandum of Association

The Memorandum and Articles of Association of your company must be printed, apart from the signatures.

....

The Companies Acts 1985 to 1989   Private Company Limited by Shares

Memorandum of Association of

_____ Limited

1. The name of the Company is _____ Limited.

2. The registered office of the Company is in England and Wales.

3. The object of the Company is to carry on business as a general commercial company.

4. The liability of the shareholders is limited.

5. The share capital of the Company is [£10,000], divided into [10,000] shares of £1 each.

We, the persons named below as subscribers, wish to form a company on the terms set out in this memmorandum and we agree to take the number of shares shown opposite our respective names.

Signatures, names and addresses of subscribers	**Number of shares taken by each subscriber**
1. Signature_____	_____
Name _____	_____
Address _____	_____
2. Signature_____	_____
Name _____	_____
Address _____	_____

Total shares taken _____

_____

Dated this _____ day of _____

Witness to the above signatures

Signature _____

Name_____

Address_____

Articles of Association

These Articles are based on Table A, with several important modifications suited to the running of a small business.

Articles of Association of

_____Limited

1. Table A

Except as varied by or inconsistent with these Articles, Table A in the schedule to The Companies Act (Tables A to F) Regulations 1985, SI 1985/805 amended by SI 1985/1052 ('Table A') is to apply to the company.

2. Shareholders

2.1 The company may have one shareholder.

2.2 A vote on a resolution is to be decided by a show of hands, unless any shareholder present in person or by proxy demands a poll, whether before or after the show of hands.

2.3 A proxy can vote on a show of hands.

3. Directors

3.1 The company may have a sole director and there is to be no maximum number of directors. Regulation 64 of Table A does not apply.

3.2 All directors are entitled to receive notice of directors' meetings. The minimum notice period is seven days, unless all directors agree otherwise.

4. Allotment of shares

The directors have general and unconditional authority to allot ordinary shares of £1 each in the capital of the company up to a maximum amount of £10,000. This authority continues for five years from the date on which these Articles are adopted. The directors do not have authority to create any other class of shares. Share certificates do not require a seal.

5. Transfer of shares

5.1 A shareholder ('the seller') intending to transfer shares ('the sale shares') is to give written notice of their intention ('the transfer notice') to the directors. The transfer notice is to specify the number of the sale shares and the seller's proposed price for them.

5.2 By virtue of the transfer notice, the seller is deemed to appoint the directors as the seller's agent for purposes of transfer of the sale shares.

5.3 Within 14 days of receiving the transfer notice, the directors are to give written notice ('offer notice') to shareholders (other than the seller) offering each of them the sale shares as nearly as possible in proportion to their existing shareholdings. Where an equal division is impossible, the directors may offer any remaining sale shares to shareholders in whatever proportions the directors decide. The offer notice is to state:

5.3.1 the total number of sale shares, and the number available to the individual shareholder

5.3.2 the seller's proposed price per sale share

5.3.3 what the shareholder is to do if that shareholder does not agree the price per share, and the time limit for doing so

5.3.4 what the shareholder must do to buy all or some of the sale shares offered to them, and the time limit for doing so.

5.4 If any shareholder does not agree the seller's proposed price per share that shareholder is, within 14 days of receiving the offer notice, to give written notice of objection ('notice of objection') to the directors. Upon receiving a notice of objection, the directors are immediately to notify other shareholders in writing of the notice of objection.

5.5 Upon receiving a notice of objection, the directors are also immediately to instruct the company's auditor to fix a fair price per share for the sale shares (which is to be the same price for all sale shares of the same class). The auditor is to act as an expert, and the auditor's determination, which is to be made in writing, is to be final and binding. The auditor's fees are to be paid by the company. If the company does not have an auditor, the determination is to be made by an independent chartered accountant appointed by the directors. Within seven days of receiving the auditor's determination, the directors are to give shareholders written notice of the new price per share ('the amended offer notice').

5.6 A shareholder wishing to buy sale shares must give written notice ('acceptance notice') to the directors. If no notice of objection is given, the acceptance notice must be given not earlier than 15 days and not later than 28 days after the date of the offer notice. If notice of objection is given, the acceptance notice must be given not earlier than the date of the amended offer notice and not later than 28 days after the date of the amended offer notice. An acceptance notice creates a binding contract for sale and purchase of the relevant sale shares. Completion of the transfer of the relevant sale shares is to take place within 28 days of the acceptance notice.

5.7 If, after the time limit for acceptance expires, any sale shares have not been accepted, they are to be re-offered to shareholders (other than the seller) in proportion to their new shareholdings.

5.8 If there are sale shares which no shareholder wants to accept, the seller has the right to sell them to whoever will buy them and at whatever price.

5.9 A shareholder is deemed to serve an irrevocable transfer notice if that shareholder transfers or purports to transfer shares in breach of this Article, or if a bankruptcy order is made against the shareholder. Where this happens, the price of the sale shares is to be determined by the company auditor or, if there is no auditor, by an independent chartered accountant.

5.10 The pre-emption provisions in this Article do not apply:

5.10.1 to any transfer by a personal representative to any person entitled to shares under the will or intestacy of a deceased shareholder

5.10.2 on the death of a joint shareholder, to any transfer of the jointly held shares into the name of the survivor.

6.   Retirement and removal of directors

6.1 The directors do not have to retire by rotation.

6.2 A director is deemed to retire if

6.2.1 his contract of employment with the company ends

6.2.2 he is convicted of a crime of dishonesty or violence

6.2.3 he no longer has the mental capacity to manage his own affairs and a certificate to this effect is signed by two doctors.

7.   Proceedings at shareholder meetings

7.1 If the number of shareholders is more than one, two shareholders must be present to form a quorum. Otherwise, the quorum is to be one.

7.2 The chairman is not to have a second or casting vote.

7.3 The shareholders may participate in a meeting by conference telephone, video link or internet relay chatroom.

8. Proceedings at directors' meetings

8.1 If the number of directors is more than one, two directors must be present to form a quorum. Otherwise, the quorum is to be one.

8.2 The chairman is not to have a second or casting vote.

8.3 The directors may participate in a meeting by conference telephone, video link or internet relay chatroom.

8.4 If a director has disclosed an interest in writing to the company, that director can be counted in the quorum and may vote on any resolution concerning the matter in which that director has an interest.

8.5 The directors must keep minutes of all meetings either in readable form or in a form from which a readable version can be made, but they do not need to do so in bound books as long as they take precautions to prevent and detect falsification. Minutes of shareholders' meetings must be available for inspection at the company's registered office.

9. Directors' pensions, insurance and gratuities

The directors have the power to provide themselves and/or former directors, including non-executive directors, with pensions and/or insurances and/or gratuities, and they are to have the right to retain any benefit which they receive. Regulation 87 of Table A does not apply.

10. Notices

Written notices may be given by hand, by post, by fax, by e-mail or by short text message.

11. Directors' liability insurance

The directors are to have the power to effect insurance for the benefit of themselves and/or former directors against any liability which they may incur for acts or omissions while carrying out or purporting to carry out their duties.

Signatures, names and addresses of subscribers

1. Signature _____

   Name _____

   Address _____

2. Signature _____

   Name _____

   Address _____

Dated this _____day of _____

Witness to the above signatures:

   Signature _____

   Name _____

   Address _____

Table A

This table represents a 'model' set of articles and is for reference only. You do not need to send this to Companies House. The preceding Articles of Association show how this table has been modified to make it more suitable for a small business.

Table A to The Companies Act 1985

Table A to The Companies (Tables A to F) Regulations 1985 (SI 1985 805) as amended by The Companies (Tables A to F) (Amendment) Regulations 1985 (SI 1985 1052).

Regulations for Management of a Company Limited by Shares

INTERPRETATION

1.   In these regulations:

'the Act' means The Companies Act 1985 including any statutory modification or re-enactment thereof for the time being in force.

'the articles' means the articles of the company.

'clear days' in relation to the period of a notice means that period excluding the day when the notice is given or deemed to be given and the day for which it is given or on which it is to take effect.

'executed' includes any mode of execution.

'office' means the registered office of the company.

'the holder' in relation to shares means the member whose name is entered in the register of members as the holder of the shares.

'the seal' means the common seal of the company.

'secretary' means the secretary of the company or any other person appointed to perform the duties of the secretary of the company, including a joint, assistant or deputy secretary.

'the United Kingdom' means Great Britain and Northern Ireland.

Unless the context otherwise requires, words or expressions contained in these regulations bear the same meaning as in the Act but excluding any statutory modification thereof not in force when these regulations become binding on the company.

SHARE CAPITAL

2. Subject to the provisions of the Act and without prejudice to any rights attached to any existing shares, any share may be issued with such rights or restrictions as the company may by ordinary resolution determine.

3. Subject to the provisions of the Act, shares may be issued which are to be redeemed or are to be liable to be redeemed at the option of the company or the holder on such terms and in such manner as may be provided by the articles.

4. The company may exercise the powers of paying

commissions conferred by the Act. Subject to the provisions of the Act, any such commission may be satisfied by the payment of cash or by the allotment of fully or partly paid shares or partly in one way and partly in the other.

5. Except as required by law, no person shall be recognised by the company as holding any share upon any trust and (except as otherwise provided by the articles or by law) the company shall not be bound by or recognise any interest in any share except an absolute right to the entirety thereof in the holder.

SHARE CERTIFICATES

6. Every member, upon becoming the holder of any shares, shall be entitled without payment to one certificate for all the shares of each class held by him (and, upon transferring a part of his holding of shares of any class to a certificate for the balance of such holding) or several certificates each for one or more of his shares upon payment for every certificate after the first of such reasonable sum as the directors may determine. Every certificate shall be sealed with the seal and shall specify the number, class and distinguishing numbers (if any) of the shares to which it relates and the amount or respective amounts paid up thereon. The company shall not be bound to issue more than one certificate for shares held jointly by several persons and delivery of a certificate to one joint holder shall be a sufficient delivery to all of them.

7.   If a share certificate is defaced, worn-out, lost or destroyed, it may be renewed on such terms (if any) as to evidence and indemnity and payment of the expenses reasonably incurred by the company in investigating evidence as the directors may determine but otherwise free of charge and (in the case of defacement or wearing-out) on delivery up of the old certificate.

LIEN

8.   The company shall have a first and paramount lien on every share (not being a fully paid share) for all moneys (whether presently payable or not) payable at a fixed time or called in respect of that share. The directors may at any time declare any share to be wholly or in part exempt from the provisions of this regulation. The company's lien on a share shall extend to any amount payable in respect of it.

9.   The company may sell in such manner as the directors determine any shares on which the company has a lien if a sum in respect of which the lien exists is presently payable and is not paid within fourteen clear days after notice has been given to the holder of the share or to the person entitled to it in consequence of the death or bankruptcy of the holder, demanding payment and stating that if the notice is not complied with the shares may be sold.

10.   To give effect to a sale the directors may authorise some person to execute an Instrument of transfer of the shares sold to, or in accordance with the

directions of, the purchaser. The title of the transferee to the shares shall not be affected by any irregularity in or invalidity of the proceedings in reference to the sale.

11. The net proceeds of the sale, after payment of the costs, shall be applied in payment of so much of the sum for which the lien exists as is presently payable, and any residue shall (upon surrender to the company for cancellation of the certificate for the shares sold and subject to a like lien for any moneys not presently payable as existed upon the shares before the sale) be paid to the person entitled to the shares at the date of the sale.

CALLS ON SHARES AND FORFEITURE

12. Subject to the terms of allotment, the directors may make calls upon the members in respect of any moneys unpaid on their shares (whether in respect of nominal value or premium) and each member shall (subject to receiving at least fourteen clear days' notice specifying when and where payment is to be made) pay to the company as required by the notice the amount called on his shares. A call may be required to be paid by instalments. A call may, before receipt by the company of any sum due thereunder, be revoked in whole or in part and payment of a call may be postponed in whole or part. A person upon whom a call is made shall remain liable for calls made upon him notwithstanding the subsequent transfer of the shares in respect whereof the call was made.

13. A call shall be deemed to have been made at the time when the resolution of the directors authorising the call was passed.

14. The joint holders of a share shall be jointly and severally liable to pay all calls in respect thereof.

15. If a call remains unpaid after it has become due and payable the person from whom it is due and payable shall pay interest on the amount unpaid from the day it became due and payable until it is paid at the rate fixed by the terms of allotment of the share or in the notice of the call, or if no rate is fixed, at the appropriate rate (as defined by the Act) but the directors may waive payment of the interest wholly or in part.

16. An amount payable in respect of a share on allotment or at any fixed date whether in respect of nominal value or premium or as an instalment of a call, shall be deemed to be a call and if it is not paid the provisions of the articles shall apply as if that amount had become due and payable by virtue of a call.

17. Subject to the terms of allotment, the directors may make arrangements on the issue of shares for a difference between the holders in the amounts and times of payment of calls on their shares.

18. If a call remains unpaid after it has become due and payable the directors may give to the person from whom it is due not less than fourteen clear days' notice requiring payment of the amount unpaid together with any interest which may have

accrued. The notice shall name the place where payment is to be made and shall state that if the notice is not complied with the shares in respect of which the call was made will be liable to be forfeited.

19. If the notice is not complied with any share in respect of which it was given may, before the payment required by the notice has been made be forfeited by a resolution of the directors and the forfeiture shall include all dividends or other moneys payable In respect of the forfeited shares and not paid before the forfeiture.

20. Subject to the provisions of the Act, a forfeited share may be sold, re-allotted or otherwise disposed of on such terms and in such manner as the directors determine either to the person who was before the forfeiture the holder or to any other person and at any time before sale, re-allotment or other disposition the forfeiture may be cancelled on such terms as the directors think fit. Where for the purposes of its disposal a forfeited share is to be transferred to any person the directors may authorise some person to execute an instrument of transfer of the share to that person.

21. A person any of whose shares have been forfeited shall cease to be a member in respect of them and shall surrender to the company for cancellation the certificate for the shares forfeited but shall remain liable to the company for all moneys which at the date of forfeiture were presently payable by him to the company in respect of those shares with interest

at the rate at which interest was payable on those moneys before the forfeiture or, if no interest was so payable, at the appropriate rate (as defined in the Act) from the date of forfeiture until payment but the directors may waive payment wholly or in part or enforce payment without any allowance for the value of the shares at the time of forfeiture or for any consideration received on their disposal.

22. A statutory declaration by a director or the secretary that a share has been forfeited on a specified date shall be conclusive evidence of the facts stated in it as against all persons claiming to be entitled to the share and the declaration shall (subject to the execution of an instrument of transfer if necessary) constitute a good title to the share and the person to whom the share is disposed of shall not be bound to see to the application of the consideration if any, nor shall his title to the share be affected by any irregularity in or invalidity of the proceedings in reference to the forfeiture or disposal of the share.

TRANSFER OF SHARES

23. The instrument of transfer of a share may be in any usual form or in any other form which the directors may approve and shall be executed by or on behalf of the transferor and, unless the share is fully paid, by or on behalf of the transferee.

24. The directors may refuse to register the transfer of a share which is not fully paid to a person of

whom they do not approve and they may refuse to register the transfer of a share on which the company has a lien. They may also refuse to register a transfer unless:

(a) it is lodged at the office or at such other place as the directors may appoint and is accompanied by the certificate for the shares to which it relates and such other evidence as the directors may reasonably require to show the right of the transferor to make the transfer;

(b) it is in respect of only one class of shares; and

(c) it is in favour of not more than four transferees.

25. If the directors refuse to register a transfer of a share, they shall within two months after the date on which the transfer was lodged with the company send to the transferee notice of the refusal.

26. The registration of transfers of shares or of transfers of any class of shares may be suspended at such times and for such periods (not exceeding thirty days in any year) as the directors may determine.

27. No fee shall be charged for the registration of any instrument of transfer or other document relating to or affecting the title to any share.

28. The company shall be entitled to retain any instrument of transfer which is registered, but any

instrument of transfer which the directors refuse to register shall be returned to the person lodging it when notice of the refusal is given.

TRANSMISSION OF SHARES

29. If a member dies the survivor or survivors where he was a joint holder, and his personal representatives where he was a sole holder or the only survivor of joint holders, shall be the only persons recognised by the company as having any title to his interest; but nothing herein contained shall release the estate of a deceased member from any liability in respect of any share which had been jointly held by him.

30. A person becoming entitled to a share in consequence of the death or bankruptcy of a member may, upon such evidence being produced as the directors may properly require, elect either to become the holder of the share or to have some person nominated by him registered as the transferee. If he elects to become the holder he shall give notice to the company to that effect. If he elects to have another person registered he shall execute an instrument of transfer of the share to that person. All the articles relating to the transfer of shares shall apply to the notice or instrument of transfer as if it were an instrument of transfer executed by the member and the death or bankruptcy of the member had not occurred.

31. A person becoming entitled to a share in consequence of the death or bankruptcy of a

member shall have the rights to which he would be entitled if he were the holder of the share, except that he shall not, before being registered as the holder of the share, be entitled in respect of it to attend or vote at any meeting of the company or at any separate meeting of the holders of any class of shares in the company.

ALTERATION OF SHARE CAPITAL

32. The company may by ordinary resolution:

    (a)   increase its share capital by new shares of such amount as the resolution prescribes;

    (b)   consolidate and divide all or any of its share capital into shares of larger amount than its existing shares;

    (c)   subject to the provisions of the Act, sub-divide its shares, or any of them into shares of smaller amount and the resolution may determine that, as between the shares resulting from the sub-division, any of them may have any preference or advantage as compared with the others; and

    (d)   cancel shares which, at the date of the passing of the resolution, have not been taken or agreed to be taken by any person and diminish the amount of its share capital by the amount of the shares so cancelled.

33. Whenever as a result of a consolidation of shares any members would become entitled to fractions of a share, the directors may, on behalf of those

members, sell the shares representing the fractions for the best price reasonably obtainable to any person (including, subject to the provisions of the Act, the company) and distribute the net proceeds of sale in due proportion among those members and the directors may authorise some person to execute an instrument of transfer of the shares to, or in accordance with the direction of the purchaser. The transferee shall not be bound to see to the application of the purchase money nor shall his title to the shares be affected by any irregularity in or invalidity of the proceedings in reference to the sale.

34. Subject to the provisions of the Act, the company may by special resolution reduce its share capital, any capital redemption reserve and any share premium account in any way.

PURCHASE OF OWN SHARES

35. Subject to the provisions of the Act, the company may purchase its own shares (including any redeemable shares) and, if it is a private company, make a payment in respect of the redemption or purchase of its own shares otherwise than out of distributable profits of the company or the proceeds of a fresh issue of shares.

GENERAL MEETINGS

36. All general meetings other than annual general meetings shall be called extraordinary general meetings.

37. The directors may call general meetings and, on the requisition of members pursuant to the provisions of the Act, shall forthwith proceed to convene an extraordinary general meeting for a date not later than eight weeks after receipt of the requisition. If there are not within the United Kingdom sufficient directors to call a general meeting, any director or any member of the company may call a general meeting.

NOTICE OF GENERAL MEETINGS

38. An annual general meeting and an extraordinary general meeting called for the passing of a special resolution or a resolution appointing a person as a director shall be called by at least twenty-one clear days' notice. All other extraordinary general meetings shall be called by at least fourteen clear days' notice but a general meeting may be called by shorter notice if it is so agreed:

   (a)   in the case of an Annual General Meeting, by all the members entitled to attend and vote thereat; and

   (b)   in the case of any other meeting by a majority in number of the members having a right to attend and vote being a majority together holding not less than ninety-five per cent in nominal value of the shares giving that right.

The notice shall specify the time and place of the meeting and the general nature of the business to be transacted and, in the case of an annual general meeting shall specify the meeting as such.

Subject to the provisions of the articles and to any restrictions imposed on any shares, the notice shall be given to all the members, to all persons entitled to a share in consequence of the death or bankruptcy of a member and to the directors and auditors.

39. The accidental omission to give notice of a meeting to, or the non-receipt of notice of a meeting by, any person entitled to receive notice shall not invalidate the proceedings at that meeting.

PROCEEDINGS AT GENERAL MEETINGS

40. No business shall be transacted at any meeting unless a quorum is present. Two persons entitled to vote upon the business to be transacted, each being a member or a proxy for a member or a duly authorised representative of a corporation, shall be a quorum.

41. If such a quorum is not present within half an hour from the time appointed for the meeting, or if during a meeting such a quorum ceases to be present, the meeting shall stand adjourned to the

same day in the next week at the same time and place or to such time and place as the directors may determine.

42. The chairman, if any, of the board of directors or in his absence some other director nominated by the directors shall preside as chairman of the meeting, but if neither the chairman nor such other director (if any) be present within fifteen minutes after the time appointed for holding the meeting and willing to act, the directors present shall elect one of their number to be chairman and, if there is only one director present and willing to act, he shall be chairman.

43. If no director is willing to act as chairman, or if no director is present within fifteen minutes after the time appointed for holding the meeting, the members present and entitled to vote shall choose one of their number to be chairman.

44. A director shall, notwithstanding that he is not a member, be entitled to attend and speak at any general meeting and at any separate meeting of the holders of any class of shares in the company.

45. The chairman may, with the consent of a meeting at which a quorum is present (and shall if so directed by the meeting), adjourn the meeting from time to time and from place to place, but no business shall be transacted at an adjourned meeting other than business which might properly have been transacted at the meeting had the adjournment not taken place. When a meeting is adjourned for fourteen days or more, at least seven

clear days' notice shall be given specifying the time and place of the adjourned meeting and the general nature of the business to be transacted. Otherwise it shall not be necessary to give any such notice.

46. A resolution put to the vote of a meeting shall be decided on a show of hands unless before, or on the declaration of the result of, the show of hands a poll is duly demanded. Subject to the provisions of the Act, a poll may be demanded:

    (a)   by the chairman; or

    (b)   by at least two members having the right to vote at the meeting; or

    (c)   by a member or members representing not less than one-tenth of the total voting rights of all the members having the right to vote at the meeting; or

    (d)   by a member or members holding shares conferring a right to vote at the meeting being shares on which an aggregate sum has been paid up equal to not less than one-tenth of the total sum paid up on all the shares conferring that right;

    and a demand by a person as proxy for a member shall be the same as a demand by the member.

47. Unless a poll is duly demanded a declaration by the chairman that a resolution has been carried or carried unanimously, or by a particular majority, or lost, or not carried by a particular majority and an entry to that effect in the minutes of the meeting

shall be conclusive evidence of the fact without proof of the number or proportion of the votes recorded in favour of or against the resolution.

48. The demand for a poll may, before the poll is taken, be withdrawn but only with the consent of the chairman and a demand so withdrawn shall not be taken to have invalidated the result of a show of hands declared before the demand was made.

49. A poll shall be taken as the chairman directs and he may appoint scrutineers (who need not be members) and fix a time and place for declaring the result of the poll. The result of the poll shall be deemed to be the resolution of the meeting at which the poll was demanded.

50. In the case of an equality of votes, whether on a show of hands or on a poll, the chairman shall be entitled to a casting vote in addition to any other vote he may have.

51. A poll demanded on the election of a chairman or on a question of adjournment shall be taken forthwith. A poll demanded on any other question shall be taken either forthwith or at such time and place as the chairman directs not being more than thirty days after the poll is demanded. The demand for a poll shall not prevent the continuance of a meeting for the transaction of any business other than the question on which the poll was demanded. If a poll is demanded before the declaration of the result of a show of hands and the demand is duly withdrawn, the meeting shall continue as if the demand had not been made.

52. No notice need be given of a poll not taken forthwith if the time and place at which it is to be taken are announced at the meeting at which it is demanded. In any other case at least seven clear days' notice shall be given specifying the time and place at which the poll is to be taken.

53. A resolution in writing executed by or on behalf of each member who would have been entitled to vote upon it if it had been proposed at a general meeting at which he was present shall be as effectual as if it had been passed at a general meeting duly convened and held and may consist of several instruments in the like form each executed by or on behalf of one or more members.

VOTES OF MEMBERS

54. Subject to any rights or restrictions attached to any shares, on a show of hands every member who (being an individual) is present in person or (being a corporation) is present by a duly authorised representative, not being himself a member entitled to vote, shall have one vote and on a poll every member shall have one vote for every share of which he is the holder.

55. In the case of joint holders the vote of the senior who tenders a vote, whether in person or by proxy, shall be accepted to the exclusion of the votes of the other joint holders; and seniority shall be determined by the order in which the names of the holders stand in the register of members.

56. A member in respect of whom an order has been made by any court having jurisdiction (whether in the United Kingdom or elsewhere) in matters concerning mental disorder may vote, whether on a show of hands or on a poll, by his receiver, curator bonis or other person authorised in that behalf appointed by that court, and any such receiver, curator bonis or other person may, on a poll, vote by proxy. Evidence to the satisfaction of the directors of the authority of the person claiming to exercise the right to vote shall be deposited at the office, or at such other place as is specified in accordance with the articles for the deposit of instruments of proxy, not less than 48 hours before the time appointed for holding the meeting or adjourned meeting at which the right to vote is to be exercised and in default the right to vote shall not be exercisable.

57. No member shall vote at any general meeting or at any separate meeting of the holders of any class of shares in the company, either in person or by proxy, in respect of any share held by him unless all moneys presently payable by him in respect of that share have been paid.

58. No objection shall be raised to the qualification of any voter except at the meeting or adjourned meeting at which the vote objected to is tendered, and every vote not disallowed at the meeting shall be valid. Any objection made in due time shall be referred to the chairman whose decision shall be final and conclusive.

59. On a poll votes may be given either personally or by proxy. A member may appoint more than one proxy to attend on the same occasion.

60. An instrument appointing a proxy shall be in writing, executed by or on behalf of the appointor and shall be in the following form (or in a form as near thereto as circumstances allow or in any other form which is usual or which the directors may approve):

PLC Limited

I/We,_____, of _____, being a member/members of the above-named company, hereby appoint _____ of _____, or failing him, _____, of _____, as my/our proxy to vote in my/our name(s) and on my/our behalf at the _____ annual/extraordinary general meeting of the company to be held on [date], and at any adjournment thereof.

_____

Signed on [date]'

61. Where it is desired to afford members an opportunity of instructing the proxy how he shall act the instrument appointing a proxy shall be in the following form (or in a form as near thereto as circumstances allow or in any other form which is usual or which the directors may approve):

PLC Limited

I/We,_____, of _____, being a

member/members of the above-named company, hereby

appoint _____ of _____, or

failing him, _____, of _____,

as my/our proxy to vote in my/our name(s) and on
my/our behalf at the _____
annual/extraordinary general meeting of the company
to be held on [date], and at any adjournment thereof.

_____

Signed on [date]'

This form is to be used in respect of the resolutions
mentioned below as follows:

    Resolution No. 1 *for *against

    Resolution No. 2 *for *against

*Strike out whichever is not desired.

Unless otherwise instructed, the proxy may vote as he
thinks fit or abstain from voting.

_____

Signed this day of [*year*]'

62. The instrument appointing a proxy and any
     authority under which it is executed or a copy of
     such authority certified notarially or in some other
     way approved by the directors may:

(a) be deposited at the office or at such other place within the United Kingdom as is specified in the notice convening the meeting or in any instrument of proxy sent out by the company in relation to the meeting not less than 48 hours before the time for holding the meeting or adjourned meeting at which the person named in the instrument proposes to vote; or

(b) in the case of a poll taken more than 48 hours after it is demanded be deposited as aforesaid after the poll has been demanded and not less than 24 hours before the time appointed for the taking of the poll; or

(c) where the poll is not taken forthwith but is taken not more than 48 hours after it was demanded be delivered at the meeting at which the poll was demanded to the chairman or to the secretary or to any director;

and an instrument of proxy which is not deposited or delivered in a manner so permitted shall be invalid.

63. A vote given or poll demanded by proxy or by the duly authorised representative of a corporation shall be valid notwithstanding the previous determination of the authority of the person voting or demanding a poll unless notice of the determination was received by the company at the office or at such other place at which the instrument of proxy was duly deposited before the

commencement of the meeting or adjourned meeting at which the vote is given or the poll demanded or (in the case of a poll taken otherwise than on the same day as the meeting or adjourned meeting) the time appointed for taking the poll.

NUMBER OF DIRECTORS

64. Unless otherwise determined by ordinary resolution the number of directors (other than alternate directors) shall not be subject to any maximum but shall be not less than two.

ALTERNATE DIRECTORS

65. Any director (other than an alternate director) may appoint any other director or any other person approved by resolution of the directors and willing to act to be an alternate director and may remove from office an alternate director so appointed by him.

66. An alternate director shall be entitled to receive notice of all meetings of directors and of all meetings of committees of directors of which his appointor is a member to attend and vote at any such meeting at which the director appointing him is not personally present and generally to perform all the functions of his appointor as a director in his absence but shall not be entitled to receive any remuneration from the company for his services as an alternate director. But it shall not be necessary to give notice of such a meeting to an alternate director who is absent from the United Kingdom.

67. An alternate director shall cease to be an alternate director if his appointor ceases to be a director; but if a director retires by rotation or otherwise but is reappointed or deemed to have been reappointed at the meeting at which he retires any appointment of an alternate director made by him which was in force immediately prior to his retirement shall continue after his reappointment.

68. Any appointment or removal of an alternate director shall be by notice to the company signed by the director making or revoking the appointment or in any other manner approved by the directors.

69. Save as otherwise provided in the articles, an alternate director shall be deemed for all purposes to be a director and shall alone be responsible for his own acts and defaults and he shall not be deemed to be the agent of the director appointing him.

POWERS OF DIRECTORS

70. Subject to the provisions of the Act, the memorandum and the articles and to any directions given by special resolution the business of the company shall be managed by the directors who may exercise all the powers of the company. No alteration of the memorandum or articles and no such direction shall invalidate any prior act of the directors which would have been valid if that alteration had not been made or that direction had not been given. The powers given by this

regulation shall not be limited by any special power given to the directors by the articles and a meeting of directors at which a quorum is present may exercise all powers exercisable by the directors.

71. The directors may by power of attorney or otherwise appoint any person to be the agent of the company for such purposes and on such conditions as they determine including authority for the agent to delegate all or any of his powers.

DELEGATION OF DIRECTORS' POWERS

72. The directors may delegate any of their powers to any committee consisting of one or more directors. They may also delegate to any managing director or any director holding any other executive office such of their powers as they consider desirable to be exercised by him. Any such delegation may be made subject to any conditions the directors may impose and either collaterally with or to the exclusion of their own powers and may be revoked or altered. Subject to any such conditions the proceedings of a committee with two or more members shall be governed by the articles regulating the proceedings of directors so far as they are capable of applying.

APPOINTMENT AND RETIREMENT OF DIRECTORS

73. At the first annual general meeting all the directors

shall retire from office and at every subsequent annual general meeting one-third of the directors who are subject to retirement by rotation or if their number is not three or a multiple of three the number nearest to one-third shall retire from office; but if there is only one director who is subject to retirement by rotation, he shall retire.

74. Subject to the provisions of the Act the directors to retire by rotation shall be those who have been longest in office since their last appointment or reappointment but as between persons who became or were last reappointed directors on the same day those to retire shall (unless they otherwise agree among themselves) be determined by lot.

75. If the company at the meeting at which a director retires by rotation does not fill the vacancy the retiring director shall if willing to act be deemed to have been reappointed unless at the meeting it is resolved not to fill the vacancy or unless a resolution for the reappointment of the director is put to the meeting and lost.

76. No person other than a director retiring by rotation shall be appointed or reappointed a director at any general meeting unless:-

   (a)   he is recommended by the directors; or

   (b)   not less than fourteen nor more than thirty-five clear days before the date appointed for the meeting notice executed by a member qualified to vote at the meeting has been given to the company of the intention to propose that person for appointment or reappointment stating the particulars which would if he were so appointed or reappointed be required to be included in the company's register of directors together with notice executed by that person of his willingness to be appointed or reappointed.

77. Not less than seven nor more that twenty-eight clear days before the date appointed for holding a general meeting notice shall be given to all who are entitled to receive notice of the meeting of any person (other than a director retiring by rotation at the meeting) who is recommended by the directors for appointment or reappointment as a director at the meeting or in respect of whom notice has been duly given to the company of the intention to propose him at the meeting for appointment or reappointment as a director. The notice shall give the particulars of that person which would, if he were so appointed or reappointed, be required to be included in the company's register of directors.

78. Subject as aforesaid, the company may by ordinary resolution appoint a person who is willing to act to be a director either to fill a vacancy or as an additional director and may also determine the rotation in which any additional directors are to retire.

79. The directors may appoint a person who is willing to act to be a director either to fill a vacancy or as an additional director, provided that the appointment does not cause the number of directors to exceed any number fixed by or in

accordance with the articles as the maximum number of directors. A director so appointed shall hold office only until the next following annual general meeting and shall not be taken into account in determining the directors who are to retire by rotation at the meeting. If not reappointed at such annual general meeting, he shall vacate office at the conclusion thereof.

80. Subject as aforesaid, a director who retires at an annual general meeting may, if willing to act, be reappointed. If he is not reappointed, he shall retain office until the meeting appoints someone in his place, or if it does not do so, until the end of the meeting.

DISQUALIFICATION AND REMOVAL OF DIRECTORS

81. The office of a director shall be vacated if:

(a) he ceases to be a director by virtue of any provision of the Act or he becomes prohibited by law from being a director; or

(b) he becomes bankrupt or makes any arrangement or composition with his creditors generally; or

(c) he is, or may be, suffering from mental disorder and either:-

(i) he is admitted to hospital in pursuance of an application for admission for treatment under the Mental Health Act 1983 or, in Scotland, an application

for admission under the Mental
Health (Scotland) Act 1960, or

(ii)   an order is made by a court having
jurisdiction (whether in the United
Kingdom or elsewhere) in matters
concerning mental disorder for his
detention or for the appointment of a
receiver, curator bonis or other person
to exercise powers with respect to his
property or affairs; or

(d)   he resigns his office by notice to the
company; or

(e)   he shall for more than six consecutive
months have been absent without permission
of the directors from meetings of directors
held during that period and the directors
resolve that his office be vacated.

REMUNERATION OF DIRECTORS

82.   The directors shall be entitled to such
remuneration as the company may by ordinary
resolution determine and, unless the resolution
provides otherwise, the remuneration shall be
deemed to accrue from day to day.

DIRECTORS' EXPENSES

83.   The directors may be paid all travelling, hotel and
other expenses properly incurred by them in
connection with their attendance at meetings of
directors or committees of directors or general

meetings or separate meetings of the holders of any class of shares or of debentures of the company or otherwise in connection with the discharge of their duties.

DIRECTORS' APPOINTMENTS AND INTERESTS

84. Subject to the provisions of the Act, the directors may appoint one or more of their number to the office of managing director or to any other executive office under the company and may enter into an agreement or arrangement with any director for his employment by the company or for the provision by him of any services outside the scope of the ordinary duties of a director. Any such appointment, agreement or arrangement may be made upon such terms as the directors determine and they may remunerate any such director for his services as they think fit. Any appointment of a director to an executive office shall terminate if he ceases to be a director but without prejudice to any claim to damages for breach of the contract of service between the director and the company. A managing director and a director holding any other executive office shall not be subject to retirement by rotation.

85. Subject to the provisions of the Act, and provided that he has disclosed to the directors the nature and extent of any material interest of his, a director notwithstanding his office:

    (a)   may be a party to, or otherwise interested in, any transaction or arrangement with the

company or in which the company is
otherwise interested;

(b)   may be a director or other officer of, or
employed by, or a party to any transaction or
arrangement with, or otherwise interested in,
any body corporate promoted by the
company or in which the company is
otherwise interested; and

(c)   shall not, by reason of his office, be
accountable to the company for any benefit
which he derives from any such office or
employment or from any such transaction or
arrangement or from any interest in any
such body corporate and no such transaction
or arrangement shall be liable to be avoided
on the ground of any such interest or
benefit.

86. For the purposes of regulation 85:

(a)   a general notice given to the directors that a
director is to be regarded as having an
interest of the nature and extent specified in
the notice in any transaction or arrangement
in which a specified person or class of
persons is interested shall be deemed to be a
disclosure that the director has an interest in
any such transaction of the nature and extent
so specified; and

(b)   an interest of which a director has no
knowledge and of which it is unreasonable
to expect him to have knowledge shall not
be treated as an interest of his.

DIRECTORS' GRATUITIES AND PENSIONS

87. The directors may provide benefits whether by the payment of gratuities or pensions or by insurance or otherwise, for any director who has held but no longer holds any executive office or employment with the company or with any body corporate which is or has been a subsidiary of the company or a predecessor in business of the company or of any such subsidiary, and for any member of his family (including a spouse and a former spouse) or any person who is or was dependent on him, and may (as well before as after he ceases to hold such office or employment) contribute to any fund and pay premiums for the purchase or provision of any such benefit.

PROCEEDINGS OF DIRECTORS

88. Subject to the provisions of the Articles, the directors may regulate their proceedings as they think fit. A director may, and the secretary at the request of a director shall, call a meeting of the directors. It shall not be necessary to give notice of a meeting to a director who is absent from the United Kingdom. Questions arising at a meeting shall be decided by a majority of votes. In the case of an equality of votes, the chairman shall have a second or casting vote. A director who is also an alternate director shall be entitled in the absence of his appointor to a separate vote on behalf of his appointor in addition to his own vote.

89. The quorum for the transaction of the business of

the directors may be fixed by the directors and
unless so fixed at any other number shall be two. A
person who holds office only as an alternate
director shall, if his appointor is not present, be
counted in the quorum.

90. The continuing directors or a sole continuing
director may act notwithstanding any vacancies in
their number, but, if the number of directors is less
than the number fixed as the quorum, the
continuing directors or director may act only for
the purpose of filling vacancies or of calling a
general meeting.

91. The directors may appoint one of their number to
be the chairman of the Board of directors and may
at any time remove him from that office. Unless he
is unwilling to do so the director so appointed
shall preside at every meeting of directors at which
he is present. But if there is no director holding
that office or if the director holding it is unwilling
to preside or is not present within five minutes
after the time appointed for the meeting the
directors present may appoint one of their number
to be chairman of the meeting.

92. All acts done by a meeting of directors or of a
committee of directors or by a person acting as a
director shall notwithstanding that it be afterwards
discovered that there was a defect in the
appointment or any director or that any of them
were disqualified from holding office or had
vacated office or were not entitled to vote be as
valid as if every such person had been duly

appointed and was qualified and had continued to be a director and had been entitled to vote.

93. A resolution in writing signed by all the directors entitled to receive notice of a meeting of directors or of a committee of directors shall be as valid and effectual as if it had been passed at a meeting of directors or (as the case may be) a committee of directors duly convened and held and may consist of several documents in the like form each signed by one or more directors; but a resolution signed by an alternate director need not also be signed by his appointor and if it is signed by a director who has appointed an alternate director it need not be signed by the alternate director in that capacity.

94. Save as otherwise provided by the articles a director shall not vote at a meeting of directors or of a committee of directors on any resolution concerning a matter in which he has directly or indirectly an interest or duty which is material and which conflicts or may conflict with the interests of the company unless his interest or duty arises only because the case falls within one or more of the following paragraphs:

(a) the resolution relates to the giving to him of a guarantee security or indemnity in respect of money lent to or an obligation incurred by him for the benefit of the company or any of its subsidiaries;

(b) the resolution relates to the giving to a third party of a guarantee security or indemnity in respect of an obligation of the company or any of its subsidiaries for which the director has assumed responsibility in whole or part and whether alone or jointly with others under a guarantee or indemnity or by the giving of security;

(c)   his interest arises by virtue of his subscribing or agreeing to subscribe for any shares, debentures or other securities of the company or any of its subsidiaries or by virtue of his being or intending to become a participant in the underwriting or sub-underwriting of an offer of any such shares, debentures or other securities by the company or any of its subsidiaries for subscription, purchase or exchange;

(d)   the resolution relates in any way to a retirement benefits scheme which has been approved or is conditional upon approval by the Board of Inland Revenue for taxation purposes.

For the purposes of this regulation an interest of a person who is for any purpose of the Act (excluding any statutory modification thereof now in force when this regulation becomes binding on the company) connected with a director shall be treated as an interest of the director and in relation to an alternate director an interest of his appointor shall be treated as an interest of the alternate director without prejudice to any interest which the alternate director has otherwise.

95. A director shall not be counted in the quorum

present at a meeting in relation to a resolution on which he is not entitled to vote.

96. The company may by ordinary resolution suspend or relax to any extent either generally or in respect of any particular matter any provision of the articles prohibiting a director from voting at a meeting of directors or of a committee of directors.

97. Where proposals are under consideration concerning the appointment of two or more directors to offices or employments with the company or any body corporate in which the company is interested the proposals may be divided and considered in relation to each director separately and (provided he is not for another reason precluded from voting) each of the directors concerned shall be entitled to vote and be counted in the quorum in respect of each resolution except that concerning his own appointment.

98. If a question arises at a meeting of directors or of a committee of directors as to the right of a director to vote the question may before the conclusion of the meeting be referred to the chairman of the meeting and his ruling in relation to any director other than himself shall be final and conclusive.

SECRETARY

99. Subject to the provisions of the Act the secretary shall be appointed by the directors for such term at such remuneration and upon such conditions as they may think fit; and any secretary so appointed may be removed by them.

MINUTES

100. The directors shall cause minutes to be made in books kept for the purpose:

    (a)   of all appointments of officers made by the directors; and

    (b)   of all proceedings at meetings of the company of the holders of any class of shares in the company and of the directors and of committees of directors including the names of the directors present at each such meeting.

THE SEAL

101. The seal shall only be used by the authority of the directors or of a committee of directors authorised by the directors. The directors may determine who shall sign any instrument to which the seal is affixed and unless otherwise so determined it shall be signed by a director and by the secretary or by a second director.

DIVIDENDS

102. Subject to the provisions of the Act the company may by ordinary resolution declare dividends in accordance with the respective rights of the members but no dividend shall exceed the amount recommended by the directors.

103. Subject to the provisions of the Act, the directors may pay interim dividends if it appears to them that they are justified by the profits of the

company available for distribution. If the share capital is divided into different classes the directors may pay interim dividends on shares which confer deferred or non-preferred rights with regard to dividend as well as on shares which confer preferential rights with regard to dividend but no interim dividend shall be paid on shares carrying deferred or non-preferred rights if at the time of payment any preferential dividend is in arrear. The directors may also pay at intervals settled by them any dividend payable at a fixed rate if it appears to them that the profits available for distribution justify the payment. Provided the directors act in good faith they shall not incur any liability to the holders of shares conferring preferred rights for any loss they may suffer by the lawful payment of an interim dividend on any shares having deferred or non-preferred rights.

104. Except as otherwise provided by the rights attached to shares, all dividends shall be declared and paid according to the amounts paid up on the shares on which the dividend is paid. All dividends shall be apportioned and paid proportionately to the amounts paid up on the shares during any portion or portions of the period in respect of which the dividend is paid; but, if any share is issued on terms providing that it shall rank for dividend as from a particular date that share shall rank for dividend accordingly.

105. A general meeting declaring a dividend may upon the recommendation of the directors direct that it

shall be satisfied wholly or partly by the distribution of assets and where any difficulty arises in regard to the distribution the directors may settle the same and in particular may issue fractional certificates and fix the value for distribution of any assets and may determine that cash shall be paid to any member upon the footing of the value so fixed in order to adjust the rights of members and may vest any assets in trustees.

106. Any dividend or other moneys payable in respect of a share may be paid by cheque sent by post to the registered address of the person entitled or if two or more persons are the holders of the share or are jointly entitled to it by reason of the death or bankruptcy of the holder to the registered address of that one of those persons who is first named in the register of members or to such person and to such address as the person or persons entitled may in writing direct. Every cheque shall be made payable to the order of the person or persons entitled or to such other person as the person or persons entitled may in writing direct and payment of the cheque shall be a good discharge to the company. Any joint holder or other person jointly entitled to a share as aforesaid may give receipts for any dividend or other moneys payable in respect of the share.

107. No dividend or other moneys payable in respect of a share shall bear interest against the company unless otherwise provided by the rights attached to the share.

108. Any dividend which has remained unclaimed for twelve years from the date when it became due for payment shall if the directors so resolve be forfeited and cease to remain owing by the company.

ACCOUNTS

109. No member shall (as such) have any right of inspecting any accounting records or other book or document of the company except as conferred by statute or authorised by the directors or by ordinary resolution of the company.

CAPITALISATION OF PROFITS

110. The directors may with the authority of an ordinary resolution of the company:-

    (a)   subject as hereinafter provided resolve to capitalise any undivided profits of the company not required for paying any preferential dividend (whether or not they are available for distribution) or any sum standing to the credit of the company's share premium account or capital redemption reserve;

    (b)   appropriate the sum resolved to be capitalised to the members who would have been entitled to it if it were distributed by way of dividend and in the same proportions and apply such sum on their behalf either in or towards paying up the amounts if any for the time being unpaid on any shares held by them respectively or in paying up in full unissued shares or debentures of the company of a nominal amount equal to that sum and allot the shares or debentures credited as fully paid to those members or as they may direct in those proportions or partly in one way and partly in the other: but the share premium account the capital redemption reserve and any profits which are not available for distribution may for the purposes of this regulation only be applied in paying up unissued shares to be allotted to members credited as fully paid;

(c)   make such provision by the issue of fractional certificates or by payment in cash or otherwise as they determine in the case of shares or debentures becoming distributable under this regulation in fractions; and

(d)   authorise any person to enter on behalf of all the members concerned into an agreement with the company providing for the allotment to them respectively credited as fully paid of any shares or debentures to which they are entitled upon such capitalisation any agreement made under such authority being binding on all such members.

NOTICES

111.Any notice to be given to or by any person

pursuant to the articles shall be in writing except that a notice calling a meeting of the directors need not be in writing.

112. The company may give any notice to a member either personally or by sending it by post in a prepaid envelope addressed to the member at his registered address or by leaving it at that address. In the case of joint holders of a share all notices shall be given to the joint holder whose name stands first in the register of members in respect of the joint holding and notice so given shall be sufficient notice to all the joint holders. A member whose registered address is not within the United Kingdom and who gives to the company an address within the United Kingdom at which notices may be given to him shall be entitled to have notices given to him at that address but otherwise no such member shall be entitled to receive any notice from the company.

113. A member present either in person or by proxy at any meeting of the company or of the holders of any class of shares in the company shall be deemed to have received notice of the meeting and where requisite of the purposes for which it was called.

114. Every person who becomes entitled to a share shall be bound by any notice in respect of that share which before his name is entered in the register of members has been duly given to a person from whom he derives his title.

115. Proof that an envelope containing a notice was properly addressed, prepaid and posted shall be

conclusive evidence that the notice was given. A notice shall be deemed to be given at the expiration of 48 hours after the envelope containing it was posted.

116. A notice may be given by the company to the persons entitled to a share in consequence of the death or bankruptcy of a member by sending or delivering it in any manner authorised by the articles for the giving of notice to a member addressed to them by name or by the title of representatives of the deceased or trustee of the bankrupt or by any like description at the address if any within the United Kingdom supplied for that purpose by the persons claiming to be so entitled. Until such an address has been supplied, a notice may be given in any manner in which it might have been given if the death or bankruptcy had not occurred.

WINDING UP

117. If the company is wound up the liquidator may with the sanction of an extraordinary resolution of the company and any other sanction required by the Act divide among the members in specie the whole or any part of the assets of the company and may for that purpose value any assets and determine how the division shall be carried out as between the members or different classes of members. The liquidator may with the like sanction vest the whole or any part of the assets in trustees upon such trusts for the benefit of the

members as he with the like sanction determines but no member shall be compelled to accept any assets upon which there is liability.

INDEMNITY

118. Subject to the provisions of the Act but without prejudice to any indemnity to which a director may otherwise be entitled every director or other officer or auditor of the company shall be indemnified out of the assets of the company against any liability incurred by him in defending any proceedings, whether civil or criminal, in which judgement is given in his favour or in which he is acquitted or in connection with any application in which relief is granted to him by the court from liability for negligence, default, breach of duty or breach of trust in relation to the affairs of the company.

Useful Contacts

Companies House

Companies House has seven offices in England, Wales and Scotland. These are

Cardiff

The Registrar of Companies
Companies House
Crown Way
Cardiff CF4 3UZ
Tel: 029 2038 8588
Central enquiries: 0870 333 3636

London

55-71 City Road
London EC1Y 1BB
Tel: 020 7253 9393

Birmingham

Central Library
Chamberlain Square Birmingham B3 3HQ
Tel: 0121 233 9047

Leeds

25 Queen Street
Leeds LS1 2TW
Tel: 0113 233 8338

Manchester

75 Mosley Street
Manchester M2 2HR
Tel: 0161 236 7500

Edinburgh

The Registrar of Companies
Companies House
37 Castle Terrace
Edinburgh EH1 2EB
Tel: 0131 535 5800

Glasgow

7 West George Street
Glasgow G2 1BQ
Tel: 0141 221 5513

Contact points

Companies House website
>www:companieshouse.gov.uk<

For leaflets, forms, name searches and links with many
other organizations, including the Inland Revenue and
the Patent Office. A session on this site could save you
a lot of telephone calls.

Electronic filing, contact Companies House Direct
Tel: 08457 573991

Same-day incorporations/change of name
Tel: 029 2038 0339

Same-day re-registration
Tel: 029 2038 0929

Policy on company names and business names
Tel: 029 2038 0362

Mortgages
Tel: 029 2038 0445

Public Search Room Cardiff
Tel: 029 2038 0124

Search accounts
Tel: 029 2038 0950

Postal searches
Tel: 029 2038 0898

Companies House Direct
Tel: 029 2038 0043

Microfiche queries and complaints
Tel: 029 2038 0527

Computer products
Tel: 029 2038 0142

Fax search
Tel: 029 2038 0517

Any of these services in Scotland
Tel: 0131 535 5800

London office
Tel: 020 7324 1707

Disqualified Directors' Register

Held at Companies House.
Tel: 0870 333 3636

Domain name searches

Access Nominet by way of the Companies House
website >www.companieshouse.gov.uk< or on
>http://www.nominet.net/howto/domainreg.html<

Trade Marks Index

Main website >http://www.patent.gov.uk< or access it
from the Companies House site
>www.companieshouse.gov.uk<

The Patent Office Central Enquiry Unit
Concept House
Tredegar Park
Cardiff Road
Newport
Gwent NP9 1RH
Tel: 08459 500505
E-mail: >enquires@patent.gov.uk<
Search and Advisory Service
Tel: 01633 811010
Fax: 01633 811020
E-mail: >commercialsearches@patent.gov.uk<

Companies House's Start in Business website

>http://www.startinbusiness.co.uk<

Companies House guidance booklets

Companies House produces a series of Guidance booklets as listed below.

All are free, and can be downloaded from the Companies House website:
>http://www.companieshouse.gov.uk/<

Alternatively you can apply for them by post from:

Cardiff
Stationery Section
Companies House
Cardiff CF4 3UZ
Tel: 0870 333 3636

Edinburgh
Stationery Section
Companies House
37 Castle Terrace
Edinburgh EH1 2EB
Fax: 0131 535 5820

Formation and registration

GBF1   Company Formation

GBF2   Company Names

GBF3   Business Names

Useful Contacts

Administration and management

GBA1	Directors and Secretaries Guide
GBA2	Annual Return
GBA3	Accounts and Accounting Reference Dates
GBA4	Auditors
GBA5	Late Filing Penalties
GBA6	Share Capital and Prospectuses
GBA7	Resolutions
GBA8	Company Charges and Mortgages
GBA8(S)	Company Charges (Scotland)
GBA9	Flat Management Companies

Winding-up

GBW1	Liquidation and Insolvency
GBW1(S)	Liquidation and Insolvency (Scotland)
GBW2	Strike-off, Dissolution and Restoration
GBW2(S)	Strike-off, Dissolution and Restoration (Scotland)

Other legislation

GB01	Oversea Companies
GB02	Limited Partnership Act
GB03	Newspaper Libel and Registration Act
GB04	European Economic Interest Groupings
GB05	Use of Welsh

NEW!

Limited Liability Partnership Formation and Names

Limited Liability Partnerships Administration and Management

Limited Liability Partnerships Winding Up (England and Wales)

Limited Liability Partnerships Winding Up (Scotland)

Additionally, forms are now available. All are prefixed LLP and all are available as usually from Companies House.

Index

Index

Printed in the United Kingdom by The Stationery Office Ltd, London
N113902 C5 10/02 775201 19585